PRINT CASEBOOKS 6/1984-85 EDITION
THE BEST IN COVERS & POSTERS

1984/85 Edition

PRINT CASEBOOKS 6

The Best in

COVERS & POSTERS

Written by
Teresa Reese

Published by
RC Publications, Inc.
Bethesda, MD

First published 1984 in the
United States of America
by RC Publications, Inc.
6400 Goldsboro Road
Bethesda, MD 20817

Manufactured in Hong Kong
First Printing 1984

**PRINT CASEBOOKS 6/1984-85
EDITION/THE BEST IN
COVERS & POSTERS**
Library of Congress Catalog Card
Number 75-649580
ISBN 0-915734-46-X

**PRINT CASEBOOKS 6/1984-85
EDITION**
Complete 6-Volume Set
ISBN 0-915734-40-0

RC PUBLICATIONS
President and Publisher: Howard Cadel
Vice President and Editor: Martin Fox
Art Director/Designer: Andrew P. Kner
Managing Editor: Teresa Reese
Associate Art Director: Glenn Biren
Assistant Editor: Tom Goss
Graphic Production: Linda Riess
Production Assistant: Susan Norr

Introduction

Graphics professionals have been waiting since the legendary creative hubbub of the 1960s ended for something really new to happen in design. This year's Casebook jurors in the Covers and Posters category seemed to feel that they were still waiting. A sampling of their observations: "No great innovations" . . . "Except for an occasional piece, there's been nothing exciting for the last five or six years" . . . "So many repeats; we've seen it before" . . . "I'm so sick of this neo-Constructivist stuff" . . . "Oh, not another of those stylized '20s-'30s steamships" . . . "None of the winners just killed me" . . . "Maybe we're all too jaded."

That last remark may be too harsh because, while they didn't find anything "new," the jurors did speak with respect of entries that met all or most of their criteria. These criteria were spelled out during the lunch break of the day-long session: A graphics piece must work totally so that the idea is right, the concept appropriate, and the execution elegant and beautiful on all counts—design, illustration, photography, typography, production.

In judging more than 1600 entries, the jurors found many that stumbled on one or more of these counts, with typography in general getting the lowest marks. Typical comments: "Great art dropped into a poor format" . . . "Good illustration but type inferior" . . . "Engaging graphics but poor production values" . . . "Photography and illustration weak compared to design" . . . "Typography so weak the piece falls apart."

Seymour Chwast is quoted as saying: "My work day is comprised of translating ideas into visual expression through symbolism, manipulation, transformation and exposition." The entries that best accomplished this found their way into the Casebook, as the jurors chose 47 posters or poster series (out of 635 entries), 26 magazine covers (out of 450), 18 book covers (out of 287), and eight record album covers (out of 239).

Going beyond generalities of style and execution, we can look at a few of the developments that have had an impact on the quality and quantity of today's posters and covers.

Although designed to be shown in the "art gallery of the streets," there are fewer and fewer public vantage points for poster display. Some large cities have bus shelter space and such locations as subway and commuter railway stations. But even these, along with other display areas more common nationally like airports, railway stations and buses themselves, seem to show product and commercial movie ads rather than posters. America has never gone in for the kiosks that are still available in France, Germany and Switzerland and even the messy, poster-congenial public wall has all but disappeared.

Luckily, this disappearing turf hasn't spelled the end of the resilient poster; it has moved indoors or to carefully designed display units intended for close-up viewing, usually far removed from public thoroughfares. It has become a poster-mailer and often adorns walls long after its original communication is old hat. However, the most significant development in poster display may prove to be in an area that was treated with disdain only a few years ago. Until fairly recently, fine art posters meant reproductions of fine art works or innocuous images like flowers, not gutsy "real" posters. But when the prices of prints and lithographs skyrocketed, a new type of poster collector emerged—older, more visually knowledgeable and more affluent than the typical poster fan, but still priced out of the market for fine art prints. These new collectors are buying so-called "high end" posters that retail for $30 to $75 and up, unframed, and spending more for framing than the poster price.

There are now some 30 large distributors of these posters worldwide, 12 in this country where sales increased by 60 per cent from 1981 to 1982 and were expected to post another healthy increase when the figures were in from 1983.

Whether or not the "fine art" poster field will turn out to be a significant source of opportunity for artists remains a question. But a trend in book publishing, the series, is already more than a promise. Almost every major publisher is bringing out series of different types—paperback reprints of backlist hardcover books as well as special new series in hardcover or paperback. As one art director inelegantly put it: "Everyone's series-happy these days."

Series take some of the risk out of publishing by reaching a specialized audience of people who are interested in a certain kind of book. Robert Scudellari, vice president/graphics for Random House, explains: "The mass paperback market is getting too mass. If you can't print 20-50,000, you don't put out a book. On the other hand, there are quality books that might sell only 3000 copies in a $12-$15 hardcover, probably just getting lost in the list as a separate title. But the same book might sell 15,000 copies in a trade [larger-sized, more expensive] paperback series priced at $7 or $8 to $10, well over the mass-market paperback price and well under that of the hardcover. You usually start with four titles and add to it as interested readers get to know what to expect." Thus, series give renewed life to previously published books by reaching a new public and challenge art directors to create a uniform look that will become familiar to readers without sacrificing imagination and graphic excellence.

The Casebook winners reflect another development that began in the early 1970s and has grown steadily more significant, namely, the enhanced look of the Sunday newspaper magazine supplement and the upgrading in the quality of these magazines. There are now more than 50 Sunday newspaper magazines around the country, of which at least a dozen are renowned for superior graphics. Fifteen Casebook winners, over 25 per cent of the winning covers, come from these leading Sunday magazine supplements. Westward, the magazine of the Dallas Times-Herald, and the (Cleveland) Plain Dealer Magazine account for five winners each, while the New York Times Magazine can boast three. The San Francisco Examiner's California Living had one cover chosen, as did the Home section of the Minneapolis Star and Tribune's Minnesota Guide.

Sunday magazines, because of smaller budgets than newsstand magazines, have offered a chance to illustrators who otherwise might not have been discovered for years. They also have attracted established artists who work for smaller fees in exchange for creative freedom and a chance to illustrate hard-hitting stories without the pressure of creating a cover aimed primarily at attracting buyers.

Fred Woodward, former art director of Westward and now with Texas Monthly, points out: "Since you're wrapped inside the Sunday paper, you have a captive audience and don't have to worry about hard-sell. I think illustrators feel they can take a chance, do something different. Even though these covers are produced with no newsstand considerations, the most successful ones, I feel, would work very well in that context."

The idea of creativity engendered despite, or possibly because of, low budgets has permeated the Casebooks since their beginning but has never been as evident, it seems to us, as in this edition. A scrutiny of winners in all categories reveals that, with very few exceptions, they were created on limited budgets or virtually on no budget at all. As one winner put it: "You don't need packs of money to produce a good album cover. The opposite probably is true because you have to think through your concept more carefully and use more imagination and ingenuity in carrying it out." This was certainly true of the album covers for Manhattan Transfer, the New York Philharmonic's *25 Marches,* and the *Rachmaninoff Piano Concerto No. 3,* as well as some of the book and magazine covers and nearly all the posters. Some budgets were limited by the client's resources. Others could be held down because the assignment offered a chance for artistic freedom or opportunities for self-promotion of one sort or another. In a number of cases, some or all of the creative people involved donated their efforts or worked for expenses only. These so-called "freebies" were occasioned either by the artist's desire for exposure or by the nature of the client (non-profit groups, charitable organizations, graphics associations, etc.), or both.

Among these shoestring budget solutions you don't find complicated artwork, expensive printing (many were restricted to black-and-white or lithographed with process colors), fancy paper (one poster winner was printed on a brown paper bag) or "modern" time-saving procedures (in most cases the simplest techniques were employed or, on the other hand, "just plain work" substituted for more expensive methods in achieving the high quality of production demanded by the jurors). It doesn't look as though work generated by the pencil, the pen or the judiciously used scissors is going to give way very soon to the computer.—*Teresa Reese*

Casebook Jurors

Ron Kellum

Following his graduation from Louisiana State University in 1974, Ron Kellum worked as an art director for a local ad agency in Baton Rouge. The next year, he moved to New York City to study at the School of Visual Arts. He then spent three years as a designer of covers and promotional material for Arista Records before joining RCA Records, where he has been designing album covers since 1980. Kellum also began teaching graphic design at SVA in 1981. His work has appeared in most major design annuals and shows.

Casebook Writer

Teresa Reese

Before joining the staff of PRINT, where she is projects editor, Teresa Reese was a writer and editor for UPI and publicity director of Hawthorn Books. She also worked on the rewrite desk and wrote features for the New York World Telegram & Sun, and served as assistant and editorial consultant for artist/architect Frederick Kiesler. A graduate of the University of Illinois with a BS in journalism, she was associate editor of *Print Casebooks 3* and *4* and managing editor of *Casebooks 5* and *6.* Ms. Reese is the author of *Casebooks 4: The Best in Packaging* and *Casebooks 5: The Best in Advertising.*

Louise Fili

Bill Nelson

Fred Marcellino

Steven Heller

Louise Fili has been art director of Pantheon Books since 1978, following several years as a senior designer/art director at Herb Lubalin Associates. In addition to her responsibilities at Pantheon, she designs books and book jackets for other major publishing houses, is consulting art director for Writers and Readers of London, and is an instructor at the School of Visual Arts. Ms. Fili is on the board of the New York Chapter of AIGA and her work has won acknowledgment from the New York Art Directors Club, AIGA Book Show, AIGA Cover Show, the Type Directors Club, *American Illustration,* the Society of Illustrators, PRINT, and Graphis Annual.

Illustrator Bill Nelson graduated from Richmond (Virginia) Professional Institute with a bachelor of fine arts degree, then worked for three years as an artist for Richmond Newspapers, Inc., and one year as an illustrator for the Richmond Mercury, a weekly newspaper. He began freelancing in 1974 and, since 1975, has operated as Bill Nelson, Inc. He has done illustrations and/or covers for New Times, Newsweek, the Washington Post Magazine, Time, TV Guide, Esquire, Playboy, and the Plain Dealer Magazine. Nelson has won over 100 awards and had two one-man shows of his illustration.

Fred Marcellino began his career as a fine artist. After graduating from Cooper Union and Yale University, he spent a year in Venice on a Fulbright scholarship. In the late '60s he decided to try his hand at design and illustration. The music business seemed a likely starting place, and soon provided many opportunities in record album covers. During the mid-'70s, when the recording industry became more oriented toward the West Coast, Marcellino turned to publishing, and has since won recognition as a designer/illustrator of book covers. His awards include the Grammy and the New York Art Directors gold medal. He also is a three-time winner of the American Book Award.

Steven Heller is art director of the New York Times Book Review and formerly the art director of the Times Op-Ed page and Evergreen Review. He writes regularly on illustration and illustrators for PRINT, Graphis, and Upper and Lower Case. He also contributes articles to Rocky Mountain magazine, American Book Collector, Idea and Target. Heller has curated a number of exhibitions on satirical art, including "The Art of Simplicissimus" (Goethe House), "L'Assiette au Beurre" (French Institute), and "Political Art 1970-80" (AIGA). He has written and/or edited a number of books on the graphic and satirical arts and written introductions for *Great Illustrators of Our Time* (Rizzoli) and *Political Graphics* (Abbeville).

Index

Magazines/Book Titles/Album Titles/Poster Titles

Clients/Publishers/Record Companies

Design Firms/Art Directors/Designers

Photographers/ Illustrators

Rachmaninoff: Piano Concerto No. 3

For art directors faced with that recurring test of ingenuity—the design of a record album cover whose low budget precludes the assignment of art—an all-type treatment is one of the more intriguing solutions. A good example of a felicitious type solution is the cover designed by art director Christopher Austopchuk for a CBS Master Works album of the difficult and seldom recorded Rachmaninoff Third Piano Concerto.

Using no set type, Austopchuk statted faces from old type books, with a bow to the Russian composer and the fact that the performance, by the USSR State Academic Orchestra, had originally been recorded in the Soviet Union. A strong and different type design results from the Russian flavor of the large, black letters announcing the composer, the work and the performer combined with a border and color bars in bright red on a background in shades of bronze and gray. To get the background, Austopchuk cut a piece of cardboard into jagged, geometrical shapes and moved them around on his illustration board as stencils, while he sprayed the surface with paint. He outlined the edges of some shapes with red pencil.

The Cubist feel of the background and the Constructivist look of the whole evoke the era of the concerto's introduction. "If it *is* a Constructivist look," says Austopchuk, "it's a very soft one with bold colors. It doesn't have the harshness nor what I consider the ugliness of Constructivism." He reports that the design was well accepted in the U.S. but was not as successful in Europe where the cover for this kind of album is more apt to feature a classical painting or standard photograph of the performer.

Client: CBS Records, New York City
Art director/designer: Christopher Austopchuk

Mormon Tabernacle Choir

For a CBS album of the Mormon Tabernacle Choir singing songs from the 1920s, says art director Christopher Austopchuk, "I wanted the cover to be an icon of the period when those songs were popular—something so familiar that you feel you've seen it before."

In her colored pencil and airbrush painting of an "All-American" family listening to one of those huge, "streamlined" radios from the era, Nancy Stahl gave Austopchuk his icon. Not only does her super-realistic illustration recreate details of furniture, clothes and hairstyles, it captures the innocence and optimism of an age when life was simpler. Even the bright, light pastel colors are as ingenuous as some of the lyrics in songs people were singing during the period called "the Great American Holiday." That was the decade that began as the effects of World War I were disappearing, and ended, almost to the month, with the arrival of the Great Depression.

Austopchuk was pleased because the obvious need for a wholesome, non-controversial cover was met in "just the way I wanted it to be."

Client: CBS Records, New York City
Art director/designer: Christopher Austopchuk
Illustrator: Nancy Stahl

Key Exchange

"Nice" may not sound like a boffo word, but when applied to a cover or poster by the Casebook jurors it became a supreme accolade; perhaps the tone of voice was as important as the word. About the cover for the quality mass paperback, *Key Exchange*, there was a chorus of variations of "Oh, that's *nice!*" . . . "That's very nice" . . . "That's really nice."

Key Exchange is the text of an Off-Broadway romantic comedy by Kevin Wade picked by Time magazine as one of the year's best plays. It concerns a young, unmarried couple and the problems that grow out of her request to exchange apartment keys. The story of '80s lovestyles also involves another young man with whom the couple bicycle-ride in the park.

The play was published as a Bard book, Avon's quality line. "Since the book wasn't commercial," says art director Matt Tepper, "it meant a more esoteric approach was permissible. It also meant a small print run and a low budget. And that meant the design would have to be kept in-house and might have to be just type." Tepper's concept was to "do something with three wheels." Designer Martha Sedgwick submitted several sample solutions, including an all-type treatment. "A couple of the samples might have given off the wrong signals to the reader," says Tepper. "One was a little too fantasy, one a little too mechanical." The appealing design chosen shows the seats and rear wheels of three bicycles in an interesting inter-locking relationship. As printed, with

the bikes dropped out in white from a gray-green background, neatness and simplicity are maintained despite the mandatory mass-paperback favorable quotation under the orange title on a black copy block. "I would have preferred the vibrancy of a match-color job with no screen," says Tepper, "but because of the low budget, it was ganged up in process."

Publisher: Avon Books, New York City
Art director: Matt Tepper
Designer: Martha Sedgwick

Right: Three alternate cover sketches.

WPA Guide to New York City

In one of the happiest of recent publishing ventures, Pantheon Books decided to reissue the famous WPA Guide to New York City, to see if this 1930s effort of the Federal Writers Project still possessed its old magic. Based on sales, the answer was a resounding "yes." The book went into additional printings, doing so well that Pantheon has already brought out hard and softcover reprints of WPA guides to several more cities, including Boston and Washington, and plans to reissue a number of others. The cover format designed by Louise Fili and illustrated by John Martinez for the New York guide, shown here, has been adapted successfully for the entire series.

One of the New York City volume's most surprising features is that it can still be used as a guidebook. But just as important is the period: Published in 1939 when the World's Fair was in full swing, a trolley ride cost 10 cents and a room at the Plaza $7.50, the guide has fascinating appeal for thirties buffs. It was this period flavor that Fili was after in the tissue layout she gave Martinez, a poster designer who had never done covers. Fili's design suggested horizontal and vertical type, slanted buildings and a Deco figure or figures in the foreground. The Statue of Liberty was the artist's idea. "Thanks to John's background," says Fili, "the cover has the strong poster identity that I wanted. His original cut paper colors were much brighter— yellows and blues—and we modified them after receiving the pen-and-ink drawing to

gray-blues and gray-greens for a more accurate period feeling. Other muted color combinations have worked nicely on later books in the series."

Publisher: Pantheon Books, New York City
Art director/designer/type designer: Louise Fili
Illustrator: John Martinez

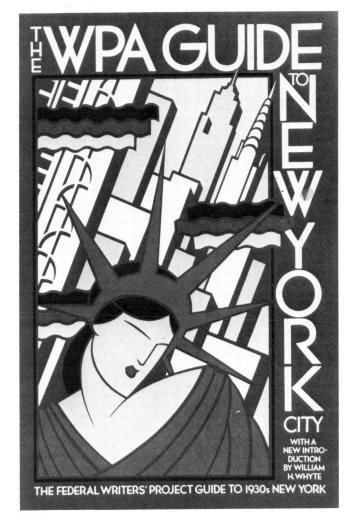

Other covers in series: Illinois (right), New Orleans (center), Washington, DC (far right).

Both time and money were limited, so Pentagram Design of London sought simple solutions for the covers of a paperback reprint series on the arts that British publisher Faber and Faber was bringing out. Perhaps the mandate for simplicity was a blessing in disguise, for it would be hard to find three cover designs that could better sum up the arts dealt with in the three books cited by the Casebook jurors.

Art director John McConnell chose clay gray as background to set off symbolic illustrations for art, music and film. A 1¼″ strip of film, cut with a jag in each end, appears in black on Rudolf Arnheim's *Film As Art*. Two musical notes making opening and closing quotation marks, placed alone in the center of the cover, symbolize *The Language of Modern Music* by Donald Mitchell. The design element for Herbert Read's *The Meaning of Art* is a question mark, the top a blue brush stroke done as a painting on a square white drop-shadowed canvas hanging on the gray "wall" of the cover. The dot at the bottom is presented as a round red sculpture on a pedestal, both casting their shadow on the wall.

The concepts were presented to the publisher's approval committee, which pronounced them appropriate for the market. This judgment was borne out in "very good" bookstore sales.

Publisher: Faber & Faber Ltd., London
Design firm: Pentagram Design,
London
Art director: John McConnell,
Designers: John McConnell, Kia Boon
Phoa

Industrial Launderer

During his almost 20 years as art director of Industrial Launderer magazine, Jack Lefkowitz has kept in mind his "invisible line" in designing sophisticated graphics for what shouldn't be, but is, an appreciative audience. Since the magazine is published by a trade association, it doesn't need excessive cover copy or hard-sell graphics. The association is made up of companies that rent uniforms and cloth cleaning supplies and, as a service, launder them.

You wouldn't think those readers would savor the simple, subtle, often abstract design that has become Lefkowitz's trademark. But consistently, in surveys conducted every two years, Industrial Launderer's readers have given the graphics high approval. Lefkowitz says he thinks it's because he never goes over the invisible line separating the too abstract from the acceptably abstract. "As long as I use realistic forms that can be recognized, the readers are satisfied and I can get away with an abstract theme behind the design."

Even so, Lefkowitz was afraid he may have stepped over the line with the cover the Casebook jurors chose. A black comb takes up the left half of the cover. Colored hairs twisting out of the comb turn into dollar signs. The reference is to the lead story about a fictitious company whose accountant went through the books with a fine-tooth comb and found hidden money, new sources of income that should figure in long-range planning. To make sure the point was taken, Lefkowitz put an illustration inside the magazine with a comb in someone's hair.

Lefkowitz, who pre-separates his line drawings for color, says he kept this cover simpler than usual because he was doing the separations by himself. He made the comb black and was able to put all of the "hairs" on one overlay and just indicate colors to the printer. He started the drawing at 5 a.m. and sent the art off to the printer by 10 a.m.

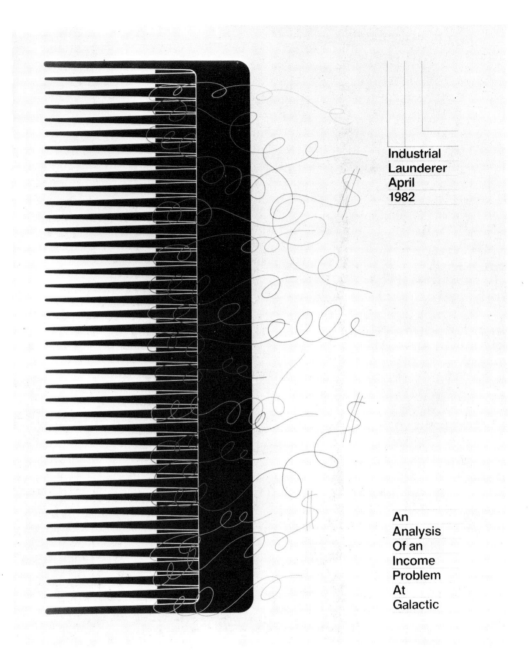

Industrial
Launderer
April
1982

An
Analysis
Of an
Income
Problem
At
Galactic

Right: Inside spread spelling out meaning of cover illustration.

An Analysis of an Income Problem At Galactic

Publisher: Institute of Industrial Launderers, Washington, DC
Art director/designer/illustrator: Jack Lefkowitz
Copywriter: David Ritchey

Minnesota Guide: Home

Before inaugurating its Minnesota Guide in time for Christmas 1982, the special advertising sections of the Minneapolis Star and Tribune were a hodge-podge of tabloid-size inserts that appeared irregularly.

The Guide, a full-size insert, would remedy that by appearing once a month with regularly scheduled sections dealing with ads for Christmas, summer, electronics, home furnishings, etc. To launch the new section with a graphic flair, the newspaper contracted with Pushpin, Lubalin, Peckolick to design covers for a number of the early issues. One of these, for the Minnesota Guide Home issue, was chosen by the Casebook jurors for its refreshing treatment of a much-worked-over subject.

The Home section deals with furniture, walls, carpets—all of the traditional products. "We had an idea," says Minnesota Guide art director David Hadley, "for a cover looking into four rooms in a building, each with a different style of furniture." But when they discussed it on the phone with Seymour Chwast, the latter, with his knack for keeping things simple, suggested that instead of whole rooms of furniture they just use four chairs, each demonstrating one style in the evolution of the chair. The client gave a go-ahead on the phone and approved the pencil sketches Pushpin sent.

The cover is divided into four panels. At upper left is Christopher Blumrich's gouache painting of a traditional post-Victorian side chair. At upper right is Elwood Smith's pen-and-ink and wash version of the comfy old chair of the '30s and '40s. At lower left is Chwast's line drawing with Cello-Tak send-up of 1950s "modren" and, next to that, Vivienne Flesher's pastel of the ubiquitous molded chair which could be metal, wood or plastic.

HOME

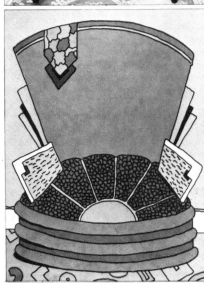

THIS MONTH'S GUIDE
ORCHESTRATING A ROOM - TWIN CITIES DESIGNERS TALK ABOUT FLOORS, WALLS, FURNITURE, WINDOWS. HOW TO MAKE THEM COME TOGETHER AESTHETICALLY TO EXPRESS THE REAL YOU. CARPETING - HOW TO BUY, WHAT TO LOOK FOR, NEW TRENDS AND IDEAS. AWARD WINNING ARCHITECT TOM ELLISON ANSWERS YOUR QUESTIONS ABOUT ENERGY EFFICIENT HOMES. WHAT'S NEW IN DECORATING BATHROOMS AND KITCHENS, BUYER'S GUIDES, AND MORE.

Client: Minneapolis Star and Tribune, Minneapolis
Design firm: Pushpin, Lubalin, Peckolick, New York City
Art director: David Hadley
Designers: David Hadley, Roger Scophammer
Illustrators: Seymour Chwast, Vivienne Flesher, Christopher Blumrich, Elwood Smith

In spring of 1982, Dugald Stermer redesigned the San Francisco Examiner's Sunday magazine, California Living, and has since served as consulting designer. It's hard to judge reader reaction to a specific cover, he says, because it's tucked inside the rest of the newspaper and doesn't account for newsstand sales. About the cover chosen by the Casebook jurors, Stermer says, "I was pleased with the result. The editor liked it. The letters, such as there were, expressed approval. People rarely write in to say they *didn't* like a cover."

The cover referred to an article called "The Vanishing Nurse: Why She Has Become an Endangered Species." The story reviewed the reasons for the shortage of nurses—hard work, low pay compared to doctors, and the increasing lack of respect for their profession.

Working from the manuscript and photographs from the newspaper's morgue, Stermer drew a nurse that he felt symbolized the profession, but a ghostly nurse whose head is eerily beginning to disappear. Stermer did his illustration with semi-soft pencil on watercolor paper and then applied watercolors. Pale blue and gray create an other-worldly feeling. The only way he could get the nurse to begin vanishing, so you could read what supposedly was behind her head, was to incorporate the logo (which he had designed in the first place), cover lines, date and other normally typeset material into the illustration.

Publisher: San Francisco Examiner/ California Living; Harold Silverman, editor
Art directors/designers: Dugald Stermer, Bill Prochnow
Illustrator: Dugald Stermer

Eisenstein at Work

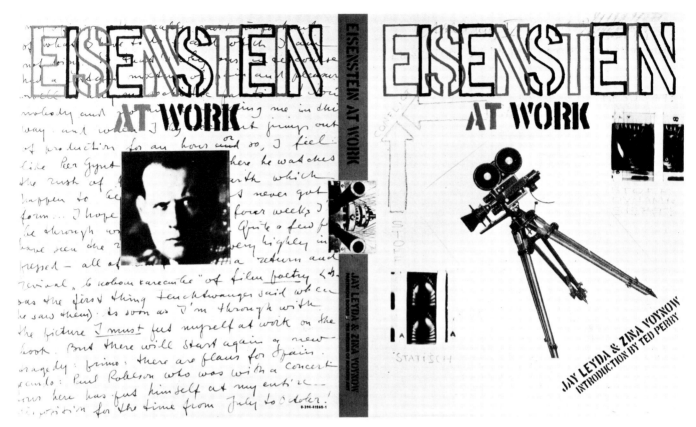

Book jackets are usually designed early so they can be used as a selling tool before the appearance of the sales brochure, which contains proofs of the jacket and pages from the book. In the case of Pantheon's *Eisenstein at Work,* however, the sales brochure preceded the jacket and used images on its cover that came from inside the book, a volume filled not only with photographs, but with original designs, drawings, and shooting plans from the hand of the great Russian filmmaker of the '20s and '30s.

"The jacket was an easy spin-off from the brochure," says Robert Scudellari, vice-president/graphics of Random House, under whose umbrella Pantheon operates as a division. The book was published in connection with the Museum of Modern Art and the museum was originally responsible for its graphics. "However," says Scudellari, "Pantheon rejected MOMA's layouts and asked my department to create a new format and design." By then, it was time to put the sales brochure together, and Scudellari designed a cover based on an Eisenstein photo montage from the book that included a vintage camera, pieces of film, and hand-printed instructions from the filmmaker.

Inside the brochure were book page proofs showing other pictures and drawings whose visual influences affected the eventual jacket design. For that, Scudellari used the brochure cover art on the front and a small photo from the film *Potemkin* on the spine. The back of the jacket is covered with a letter in the filmmaker's handwriting (in English, curiously enough) on which a striking photo of a youthful Eisenstein is superimposed. The title is stenciled in red and black.

Scudellari wanted to give the cover a hand-made look reminiscent of Russian graphics of the early 1900s. "After some trouble," he reports, "we found a tan laid paper like that used in Eisenstein's time. Stencil lettering was perfect because it hasn't changed in this century; hand-lettering just went into the deep freeze when photo techniques came along. The Russian Constructivists all hand-lettered or painted their type."

Publisher: Pantheon Books, New York City
Art director/designer/letterer: R.D. Scudellari

HENRY MILLER

TROPIC OF CANCER

MODERN LIBRARY

HENRY JAMES

THE PORTRAIT
OF A LADY

MODERN LIBRARY

Modern Library, the still-low-priced granddaddy of hardcover reprint books, has been redesigned many times during the almost 70 years it has existed, first in England, and, since 1925, in America where it was incorporated by Bennett Cerf and Donald Klopfer, founders of Random House. Robert Scudellari, vice-president/graphics, has been involved in four Modern Library redesigns since he joined Random House in the mid-'60s. The latest format, he says, has the classical look "the editorial people wanted." On tan laid paper, Scudellari combined black type with the book title

dropped out of Chinese red panels on the jacket front and spine. The illustrations are woodcuts by Stephen Alcorn, who did 15 titles, including the four Casebook winners, during 1983 and was scheduled to complete the artwork for 24 additional titles during 1984. The four covers shown here inaugurated the new design.

"I saw Alcorn's portfolio of 30 or 40 woodcuts of artists in Upper & Lower Case," Scudellari recalls, "and thought what he was doing would be very suitable, reminiscent of Rockwell Kent's wood engravings during Modern Library's formative years in the

1920s." Scudellari's favorite among the first four is the highly stylized, but simple, woodcut of Henry Miller for the cover of *Tropic of Cancer*. The lace curtain background and elaborate hat of the woman in an oval picture frame suggest the period of Henry James's *Portrait of a Lady*. Then there is what Scudellari calls a Picasso-ish portrait of Joseph Conrad with a background suggesting the tropical setting of *Nostromo*. The Art Nouveau carving for Jerzy Kosinski's *The Painted Bird* is a mass of curving complexities in the style of Aubrey Beardsley. "It's interesting to see how Alcorn's

work has grown with each illustration," Scudellari observes. "The early ones were individual portraits, while later cuts create more of a scene and project the atmosphere of the book."

Unfortunately, Scudellari confesses, the paper stock does not wear well, on a long-term basis, and a lamination process is being considered.

JOSEPH CONRAD

NOSTROMO

MODERN LIBRARY

JERZY KOSINSKI

THE PAINTED BIRD

MODERN LIBRARY

Right: Woodcut of Vincent Van Gogh from artist Stephen Alcorn's portfolio. Graphic concept for Modern Library jacket redesign grew out of Alcorn's portfolio of portraits of famous artists.

VAN GOGH

Publisher: Modern Library, New York City
Art director/designer: R. D. Scudellari
Illustrator: Stephen Alcorn

Pantheon has an impressive backlist of quality European fiction, much of it a legacy of Helen and Kurt Wolff, who founded the company when they came to this country just before World War II. Although the Wolffs took a number of famous authors with them when they sold Pantheon to Random House in the '60s and went to Harcourt Brace, there remained behind many other authors whose books had moderate to good sales in hardcover. Books like these lend themselves to reissue in paperback, usually in an appropriate series such as Pantheon's Modern Classics. Covers of the first four books in this series were Casebook winners.

"Series have always been a welcome challenge to me," says art director Louise Fili. "I try each time to create a look entirely new to paperback. For these, I used a matte stock (Navajo) and asked Dagmar Frinta to do the illustrations because I thought her elegant, literary, European direction would be perfect." To achieve a cohesive look for the first four books, a grid was established in which the main character would be sitting in the foreground with some appropriate small object, while a suitable background element would reinforce the sense of the illustration.

For Giuseppe di Lampedusa's *The Leopard*, the background element was the rear of a leopard, "the royal rule of the Sicilians," leaving the picture. Frinta put a thistle in the foreground for Yashar Kemal's *Memed, My Hawk* because the hero, although a revolutionary, had a defensive, not offensive, stance, "like the thistle which

PANTHEON MODERN CLASSICS

Young Törless

R O B E R T   M U S I L

PANTHEON MODERN CLASSICS

The Story of a Life

K O N S T A N T I N   P A U S T O V S K Y

won't prick you if you leave it alone; you only get hurt if you disturb it." Equally apt symbols express the theme of the other two books, *The Story of a Life* by Konstantin Paustovsky and Robert Musil's *Young Törless*.

Frinta's work here is a departure from previous technique and style. The figures, although arresting and richly textured, are not as stylized and whimsical as in her past work. Instead of drawing and coloring on sepia paper, her method here involves drawing in pen-and-ink, then working in watercolor and hand-made cut paper in unusual colors. With paper accounting for large areas of flat color, the whole piece is essentially a jigsaw in which various parts are drawn, colored and pasted down separately. "This technique gives me a lot of freedom," Frinta says. "If I make a mistake or want to change something, I don't ruin the entire drawing."

Fili combined Frinta's illustrations with scratchy calligraphic logotype titles. She had meant only to indicate the look she wanted when she comped the first book, but, she says, "I found that no one else could carry out the same style, so I was stuck with the job myself." She wrote the title "50 or 100 times" in very small letters on blotter paper with a "ratty" crow quill pen, then blew the titles up on a stat, chose the best letters and pieced them together. "We must go to great pains," she laughs, "to simulate spontaneity."

Publisher: Pantheon Books, New York City
Art director/designer/letterer: Louise Fili
Illustrator: Dagmar Frinta

"This is a newspaper supplement stuffed in a Sunday paper with a lot of color advertising inserts," says art director Greg Paul, referring to the Cleveland Plain Dealer Magazine. "We always tried to stand apart from them." Not only did the magazine sections Paul designed stand apart from the advertising inserts, they stood apart from virtually all of the other Sunday newspaper magazines published around the country, bringing recognition and awards to the Plain Dealer. For example, the Casebook jurors picked no fewer than five of Paul's covers.

The cover for May 2, 1982, was a rush job which Paul solved by using an existing piece of art. The topic was "Full Moon: Madness and Myth." Paul had a copy of the manuscript, a briefing from the editor and one week to produce a cover. "I remembered having seen a compelling 'moon face' in an old Hellman Design Studio calendar," he says. "I couldn't find a copy, so I called Hellman and they put me in touch with the artist, Nancy Niles. She sent a 4-by-5 transparency of the art. I was ill the day the cover was going to the printer, so I described the layout and color choices over the phone to an assistant." Despite its rocky road, Paul was satisfied with the cover's outcome. "I'd always liked that image and was pleased to find an appropriate use for it."

Paul had more time, three weeks, "enough to do things right and not rush it," he says, for the September 26, 1982, cover involving the touchy subject of crime and Cleveland's gay community. Called

"Cruising Scared," the story detailed the dangers that gays face at the hands of hostile strangers. "Photographer Steve Hill was very much involved with me in formulating the solution," says Paul. "I think we found a tasteful way to present the subject without pulling any punches."

The chilling cover photo shows the back of a man clad in leather pants, naked to the waist, and the knife he is holding behind him, ready to stab a victim who is represented only by his hands embracing his would-be assailant. The simple, dramatic, symbolic photo was one of many poses Paul and Hill tried. In some others, the model was wearing jeans rather than the ominous leather pants of the selected photo. Some were discarded as "too suggestive" or because a smaller knife was not as graphic, or a chain in the hands of the attacker was not considered immediate enough.

There were four weeks, time to do a complicated photographic production shot, for the cover of November 21, 1982. Paul received a briefing from the editor on the story, a first-person account of a woman who went into a deep coma after an auto accident injury and gradually regained consciousness over a period of months. "We wanted," says Paul, "to show the fear and alienation and confusion she described."

A hospital room set was built in photographer Robert Holcepl's studio, the bed on loan from a local hospital. The final print was a double-exposure done in the enlarger from two negatives, one of the

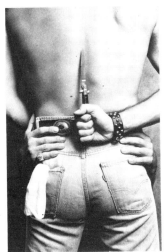

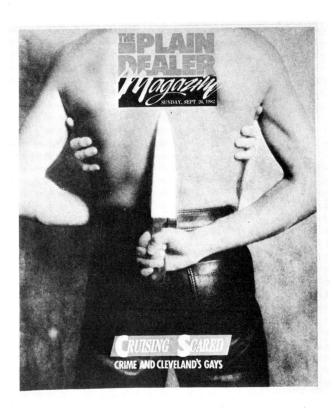

Top left: Original black-and-white cover photograph. Three other photos shown were rejected because (top center) "the chain is graphic but not immediate enough," (lower left) "pose is too suggestive," and (lower center) "hands are too octopus-like and small knife not graphic enough."

room with an empty bed, the other of the model lying in a white box cut to the size of the bed and filled with dry-ice vapor fed from a hose inserted in a hole in the bottom of the box. The final picture visualizes the woman's feeling of alienation from her own body as she went through periods of marginal consciousness. "The original photo print was perfect," Paul reports, "but the printing was poor and subtlety and impact were lost."

The cover for the 1983 Valentine's Day issue was a simple, "hitchless" operation. The story was entitled "Why Do Fools Fall in Love?" and dealt with people's needs for loving, nurturing relationships. Lead time was five weeks. In a sketch book that Brad Holland had sent him for reference, Paul found a pen-and-ink drawing of a couple wearing heart-shaped masks. "I knew the concept was perfect for our cover," says Paul, "and commissioned Brad to do it as a color painting. It turned out as I had hoped—romantic looking but a little bit cynical as well." Suffused in a rosy glow, the almost monochromatic, subtle color scheme of Holland's acrylic painting gives it a classic, timeless feeling that befits the venerable holiday.

About the cover for the April 3, 1983, Easter issue, Paul says, "We did it in a hurry." He had a briefing from the editor and writer on a story about priests leaving the priesthood ("Following the Call to a New Vocation.") "I thought this was another good assignment for Bob Holcepl, a photographer I work with a lot," says Paul. "When I describe a shot to him

I find that when I arrive he's got everything set up just the way I saw it. We're sort of on the same wave-length." Paul wanted to show that the decision to leave the priesthood is painful, creating an emotional loss for priests that "removes a piece of themselves." A photographer's assistant was posed in a priest's habit, while a second assistant held a detachable collar in front as though he were pulling it from his neck. The photo retoucher extended the background to delete the neck, making it look as though it had been cut out. Paul reports that some readers were upset to see this image on Easter Sunday.

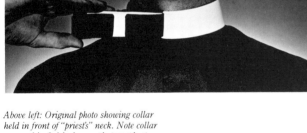

Above left: Original photo showing collar held in front of "priest's" neck. Note collar removed in finished cover photograph at top. Above right: Pen-and-ink sketch for Valentine's Day cover.

Client: The Plain Dealer Publishing Co., Cleveland
Art director/designer: Greg Paul
Illustrators: Nancy Niles (May 2, 1982), Brad Holland (February 13, 1983)
Photographers: Robert Holcepl (November 21, 1982; April 3, 1983), Steve Hill (September 26, 1982)
Retoucher: David Luciano (November 21, 1982; April 3, 1983)

Time

Time's policy of using fine artists for an occasional cover goes back to the days of Henry Luce, who liked the idea but pointed out that a news magazine could hardly indulge itself in this practice week after week. Some notable covers by fine artists through the years have been George Segal's environmental sculpture for the computer as Machine of the Year in 1982, Will Barnett's chess game for a story on the arms talks, and Jim Dine's portrait of Lech Walesa.

For this Casebook, the jurors chose the Time cover of October 18, 1982, celebrating John Updike's 50th birthday with a painting by Alex Katz. Art director Rudy Hoglund had more freedom with funds than usual and more advance notice of the topic than is generally available on a weekly. Despite the generous schedule, the time spent by the artist with the subject was limited to a few days. Katz had three one-and-a-half-hour sittings with Updike for the oil-on-canvas portrait.

This was Time's second cover on Updike. The first, 15 years ago, was a realistic portrait by Robert Vickrey. The 1982 story dealt with Updike as a successful author in middle age. Katz was selected for the "kind of warmth and vigor" he would bring to the portrait, cover-titled "Going Great at 50."

Katz, who probably has a surer graphic sense than any other fine artist painting today, gives us Updike in pastels, his hair a thatch of gray, against a country landscape of green grass and a tree in leaf. The configurations of the elongated back of the head, pink shadow on the face, pink shirt, black tie with gray and yellow stripes, and large diagonals in the herringbone tweed of the jacket form a series of geometrics that keep the viewer's eye moving in every direction.

Asked whether the spring-like green leaves (in October) and pastel colors, with their oblique resemblance to a New Yorker magazine cover, were,

perhaps, a tongue-in-cheek reference to the fact that Updike has been associated with New Yorker throughout his writing career, Katz replied, "It never once entered my mind."

The cover did well at the newsstands although Updike's face, despite his fame, is not familiar to the general public, even to many people who have read his work.

Publisher: Time Inc., New York City
Art director: Rudy Hoglund
Artist: Alex Katz

The Joke

Czech author and émigré Milan Kundera was a hot literary property after his novel *The Book of Laughter and Forgetting* elicited critical acclaim and he won the Commonwealth Award, given, like the Nobel Prize, for total literary output rather than for one work. To take advantage of heightened reader interest, Harper & Row decided to reprint Kundera's first novel, *The Joke*, in a new and better translation.

The book is set in Communist Czechoslovakia and was printed there during the thaw that preceded the Russian crackdown in August 1968. After that, Kundera's books were banned; he left in 1975 and now lives in Paris. *The Joke* concerns an iconoclastic free-thinker who sends a postcard to a young woman he loves, on which, in jest, he makes disparaging comments about party politics. He is in deep trouble after the postcard is intercepted, and that's what the book is about.

For his cover, designer/illustrator Fred Marcellino wanted to convey the irony and humor of the book in a way that would say "literary" rather than "best-seller," an epithet for the commercial-looking design that combines big type with a small, spot photo. His solution is a painting in airbrush, acrylic and watercolor of a mailbox into which a hand is dropping a postcard through the top. The view of the inside of the mailbox reveals another hand reaching up from a hole in the bottom ready to grab the card. The bright blue outside contrasts with the dark interior of the mailbox, on which the title appears in a small, jokey script dropped out in white.

"I felt the image was simple and direct," says Marcellino, "while the small type and large expanse of surrounding space would set it apart from competing books."

The Joke

A Novel by The Author of THE BOOK OF LAUGHTER AND FORGETTING

MILAN KUNDERA

Publisher: Harper & Row, New York City
Art director: Joseph Montebello
Designer/illustrator: Fred Marcellino

Saki: A Life of Hector Hugo Munro

Art director Frank Metz decided that a photograph of H.H. Munro should be cover art for the first biography ever published of the British humorist, who, under the pen name Saki, chronicled upper-middle-class life in Edwardian England through a series of gracefully written, brilliantly satirical stories. Metz sent several photographs of Munro to designer Louise Fili. "They were okay," says Fili, "but not inspiring, and I didn't start work on the cover right away. Then I received an additional photograph, and it was so appropriate to the period and the subject that I knew we had our cover."

The Munro of the photo epitomizes the era he satirized with slashing wit. In it, he looks elegant, languid and just a little bit lost. Fili filled the cover with the photo, expertly hand-tinted by Beatrice Fassell, and ran the title, *Saki*, across the top, dropped out in white from the dark background and the subject's forehead.

"When I first set to work on the design," says Fili, "I found I had comped a nonexistent type. Since there was no time for hand-lettering and barely enough to set type, I re-cycled a jacket with a similar typeface that I had done earlier for Pantheon's *The Streets of Paris*, containing remarkably similar letters to the title I was working on." By re-using Eve Light Italic, Fili had the stylized, turn-of-the-century European look she wanted.

Above left: Eve Light Italic type used by art director for previous Pantheon book jacket came close to type envisioned for Saki and was thus "re-cycled."

Publisher: Simon & Schuster, New York City
Art directors: Frank Metz, Louise Fili
Designer/type designer: Louise Fili
Hand-tinting: Beatrice Fassell

Aunt Jeanne

Aunt Jeanne is the sixth Georges Simenon cover portrait that woodcut artist Bascove has done for Harcourt Brace Jovanovich. Each of her portraits has been a strong, direct characterization of the suspense novel's protagonist and, each time, the artist has used a visual symbol to suggest the individual's situation and hint at what the reader might expect.

Aunt Jeanne has a mysterious, only hinted at, past and an intense identification with the fate of her childhood home. Bascove shows the woman peering straight at us from a window of that home. Only half of the casement window is open so that part of the figure is shrouded and indistinguishable behind a lace curtain. The half-shown, half-hidden theme of the figure is repeated in the typography of the title in the same lavender and black.

"The people at HBJ seemd pleased with the cover," says Bascove, "and added a wonderfully sharp and clear printing job. The sole difficulty was my own stubbornness in feeling that a French countryside window was incomplete without a lace curtain. Carving the lace from a plank of rock maple was a bit more time-consuming than I expected."

Publisher: Harcourt Brace Jovanovich, San Diego, CA
Art director: Rubin Pfeffer
Illustrator/letterer: Bascove

The Feud

Although *The Feud* was not part of Thomas Berger's Reinhart series, designer/illustrator Fred Marcellino wanted its cover to be similar in treatment and feeling to the ones he had done for those four previous Berger books.

The Feud is about an escalating situation that begins with an inadvertent confrontation in a hardware store and develops into a full-fledged feud between two families. "Like all Berger books," says Marcellino, "it is funny, perceptive and outrageous." Marcellino's design for one of the Reinhart series, *Reinhart in Love*, shows, only from the knees down, a couple embracing; her spiky heels are digging into his feet. The other three covers had equally eccentric images, but also, in a very calculated way, gave a big play to the author's name.

When art director Jim McGuire asked Marcellino to design the cover for the latest Berger book, Marcellino felt the author's name should again be used to sell the book. He isolated the name and ran it in large, heavy, hand-drawn letters in a box that takes up the bottom third of the illustration. The rest of the space is given over to an airbrush and acrylic painting of a pie hitting a policeman in the face. The book title, in an airy sans-serif, appears on the pie tin.

"I wanted the slapstick image on the top, with light type, to contrast with the billboard of the author's name," says Marcellino, "and to let his readers know that he was still up to his old tricks."

Publisher: Delacorte Press, New York City
Art director: Jim McGuire
Designer/illustrator/type designer: Fred Marcellino

Sounding the Territory

Knopf's art director, Lidia Ferrara, gave Fred Marcellino the manuscript of Laurie Goldman's novel, *Sounding the Territory*, knowing that he would rather get his ideas from that than from pre-design conferences. Sometimes Marcellino bases his cover design on a book's story line, but more often he will try to evoke an atmosphere. This may or may not be based on a specific incident in the book, but if it is, chances are good the incident has been adapted rather than reported.

The Goldman novel is about an adolescent youth who has trouble relating to people, especially his family, and persists in destructive behavior. He tries to help himself by interacting with other disturbed people. One day, on a bus, he tries to comfort a youngster and they begin sailing paper airplanes around the vehicle.

Marcellino transformed that image to the corner of an empty room filled with paper airplanes that have missed their targets, two open windows, and landed on the floor instead. "I chose the paper airplanes," explains Marcellino, "to symbolize the tentative and failed attempts of the young main character not only to assert himself but to free himself from mental disorder and despair. The windows represent the real world, but in his immaturity the character keeps failing to connect."

The pale tan-green wall of the airbrushed painting provides a field for the bold, clean type of the book title and more delicate, serifed letters of the author's name. "The retail environment for books is so cluttered graphically," says Marcellino, "that I try for simplicity and directness."

Publisher: Alfred A. Knopf, Inc., New York City
Art director: Lidia Ferrara
Designer/illustrator: Fred Marcellino

It was poetic justice of a sort when National Lampoon commissioned comic artist Gary Hallgren to illustrate the cover of its "Do-It-Yourself" issue, a compendium of instruction that included tips on how to forge money and a stomach-churner entitled "How to Perform Hemifacial Spasm Surgery on Yourself." The assignment—brainchild of art director Michael Grossman and editor Sean Kelly—was to get as close as legally possible to Disney's Pinocchio making a do-it-yourself doll playmate. Lampoon had agreed not to use any copyrighted Disney characters after Disney threatened legal action against an early issue that featured Minnie Mouse on the cover and Disney parodies inside. Hallgren is permanently enjoined from using Disney characters because of Disney's successful 1971 suit against Air Pirates, a short-lived underground comix book put out by Hallgren and three others named in the suit.

Hallgren's airbrush and watercolor painting for Lampoon's June 1982 cover is really a do-it-yourself lesson in parodying Disney without getting into legal trouble. According to Hallgren, Disney is troublesome to parody because his images are so widely distributed in the American collective unconscious "that when they're served back up to us it becomes a closed cultural feed-back loop."

The brush and watercolor background of Hallgren's painting is pure Disney Golden Age—the Bavarian backdrop for toymaker Gepetto's workshop and the Italian folk marionette, Pinocchio, who is turned into a real boy. Hallgren says he asked himself, "If I were a wooden cartoon character, what kind of doll would I carve to become my live playmate after the lights went out?" Although Pinocchio appears to look the way we remember him, Disney never created a doll like this sex object of Hallgren's. Snow White, she isn't.

The thin black outline of the characters is 100 per cent cel animation, but now the differences with Disney emerge. The airbrush modeling of the characters, which gives the painting its unique quality, was never used by Disney. Pinocchio, whose nose, Hallgren says, is at about the "three-lie" stage, has been changed slightly, but significantly. His white shirt was changed to green, his shawl collar eliminated, bow-tie changed to a neckerchief, big blue sabots substituted for his one-strap buckled shoes, and rolled-down stockings added. Here, he has brown instead of blue eyes, thick rather than light eyebrows, and a green hat with turned-up brim replaces the original's tan, turned-down brim and red feather. The knee and elbow joint connections are more prominent on the Lampoon cover and, finally, this Pinocchio has five fingers instead of the four that Disney animators used to save thousand of strokes in a full-length animated film.

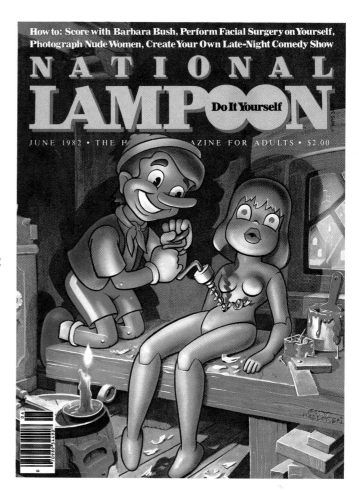

Publisher: NL Communications, Inc., New York City
Art director: Michael Grossman
Editor: Sean Kelly
Illustrator: Gary Hallgren

Good Morning Midnight

After Leaving Mr. Mackenzie

Since the novels of Jean Rhys are not typical mass-paperback fare, Fred Marcellino, who designed and illustrated their rack-size cover format for Harper & Row's Perennial Library, wanted them to stand out from garish competitors through a unique subtlety that would still convey the spirit of the books. Although not prolific, the reclusive British author has always had a small, but devoted—almost cult—audience and the popularity of her books in hardcover through the years induced the publisher to attempt to popularize them further.

The books (both published in the 1930s) whose covers were chosen by the Casebook jurors are typical of the author's subject matter—lonely, unattached women living by their wits in European cities, drifting from one man to another and alienated in the male-dominated society of their day. Marcellino says he saw the heroines of the Rhys novels as "living on the fringes of life, never having enough money, unliberated in the sense that their destiny is tied up with men. They are obsessed with fashion and appearing young. All they can offer is their looks, and when these begin to go they are frightened and unsure." Marcellino studied fashion photographs from the '30s and gave the women in his airbrush paintings a manikin look. "Because they are shadowy, half people," he says, "I wanted viewers not to know whether they were looking at manikins or women."

Marcellino placed each stylized figure, wearing a hat from the period, against a diagonally slatted background—blue for the woman (or manikin) dressed in brown, purple and tan for *After Leaving Mr. Mackenzie*, and orange and green for the brown and biege-clad figure of *Good Morning Midnight*. The artist hand-lettered the titles, white with dark drop shadows, in the kind of script the heroines might have used, thinking it chic.

Publisher: Harper & Row, New York City
Art director: Joseph Montebello
Designer/illustrator: Fred Marcellino

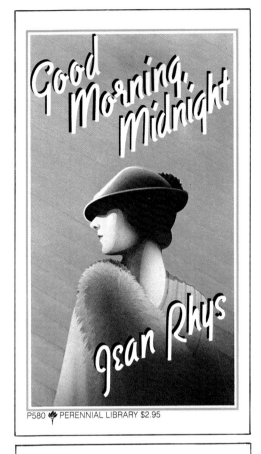

P580 ❧ PERENNIAL LIBRARY $2.95

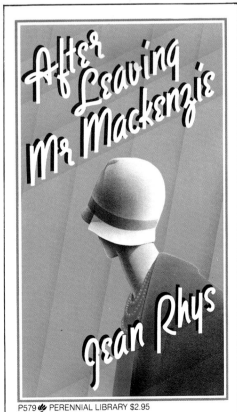

P579 ❧ PERENNIAL LIBRARY $2.95

The typical "movie book" cover usually has lots of pictures on a black background plus touches of gold and silver. A cover like this had been designed for Ethan Morrden's *Movie Star: A Look at the Women Who Made Hollywood,* scheduled for winter release by St. Martin's Press. When the sales representatives were introduced to the new list at their traditional conference, however, they, along with the editor and marketing staff, felt that Morrden was a writer of enough distinction to "break out" of the film book category. "Therefore," says art director Deborah Daly, "it was decided to scrap the cover we had and hold the book over to spring, 1983, so we could design a new one. We wanted something different and interesting, an illustration that would make the book look like a novel."

Editor Michael Denneny, says Daly, came up with the idea of a swimming pool with the Hollywood Hills in the background; "he also wanted pastel colors." Daly asked Barry Gross to do the illustration. A free-form swimming pool with greenish-turquoise water is the focus of Gross's acrylic airbrush and pastel painting in muted shades of raspberry, lavender and blues. The dusky, evening scene, with impressionistic lights in the background hills, is devoid of people, but an ashtray holding a lighted, fresh cigarette in a long holder (brush-painted, as were a few other elements needing a hard line) creates the expectancy of something about to happen. "I wanted to convey the promise of romance," says Gross. The painting, which wraps around the book, is locked firmly into the Deco period of Hollywood's heyday by Manuela Paul's title billboard on the front and spine.

Publisher: St. Martin's Press, New York City
Art director: Deborah Daly
Editor: Michael Denneny
Illustrator: Barry Gross
Type designer: Manuela Paul

Picture

Picture magazine began its career in July 1976 as a giant (13″ by 19″) photography periodical. It was started by Don Owens to "celebrate the work of photographer/artists through a gallery in magazine form." The first five beautifully printed issues came out sporadically; then Owens was joined in the publication of the next eight issues by a partner, David Gray Gardner of Gardner/Fulmer Lithography in Buena Park, California, Picture's printer from the start. Gardner assumed full ownership in 1980 and published several issues before commissioning Cross Associates to do a total redesign.

The current 11″-by-13″ format made its debut with Issue 18, whose cover, enhanced by a quietly colorful new logo, was chosen by the Casebook jurors. The new magazine is a genuine showcase for Gardner/Fulmer Lithography. "Our aim," says designer Carl Seltzer of Cross Associates, "was to give Picture an art magazine quality." A four-column grid was established, with Bodoni Book for text type and a large Bodoni photo-face for the logo, colored in shades of blue, green, purple, orange and yellow on a white background.

Also introduced was a theme for each issue. A visual pun was used on the cover of No. 18 to illustrate the theme of tableau photography. Looking as though someone had just pulled it from a Polaroid camera and tossed it down on the large white background is Don Rodan's 3″-by-3″ colored Polaroid shot of a nude, model-slim and perfectly made up woman talking on the telephone. Titled "The Muse," it is one of Rodan's Greek Myth series which also includes Cyclops (a man with a fried egg in the middle of his forehead) and Cerberus (a one-headed dog observing a checkerboard). The cover illusion was achieved by photographing a Polaroid photo frame, then stripping in Rodan's image. Drop shadows distance the photo from the background.

Left: Spread from redesigned Picture magazine of two photographs from Patrick Nagatani's "Chromo-Therapy" series.

Publisher: Picture Publishing Co., Santa Fe Springs, CA; Jean Gardner, mangaging editor
Design firm: Cross Associates, Newport Beach, CA
Art director: Jim Cross
Designer: Carl Seltzer
Photographer: Don Rodan

Champaign: How About Us?

A new band called Champaign agreed with art director Nancy Donald that they should not appear on the cover of their first album for CBS but should, instead, find an image that would symbolize their music. "We wanted the cover to say 'city'," Donald recalls, "to get across the idea of the group's urban, sophisticated, black, contemporary music. It was important to project romance and, above all, dancing."

Donald, who is based in Columbia Records' Los Angeles office, went to Chicago to meet the band and spent a day there with drummer Rocky Maffit visiting the Art Institute, Rizzoli's book and print shop and a large record store. "Maffit has a great visual sense," she reports, "and knew instinctively what was right for the music. We were able to eliminate a lot of wrong directions."

Back in Los Angeles, Donald prepared a number of comps, including abstracted city landscapes and a Roy Lichtenstein-style cartoon couple. The nod went to an illustration for a halftone process from a 1920s (by now copyright-free) book on printing techniques. The shiny black men's dress shoes, with a silk scarf and elegant address book dropped casually on the plush carpet beside them, are provocative enough to steal attention from competing albums at the retail level. Since the photo was already screened, it was re-photographed and retouched to minimize the possibility of moire. The retoucher's addition of a pearl necklace heightens interest by inserting a feminine presence. Donald airbrushed the reverse side to conform to the grainy effect on the front and echoed the main image with a tiny pair of black shoes. Her only regret concerns the type, a spaced-out condensed sans-serif in black with white drop shadows. "I just wish," she says ruefully, "that I'd made it a little bolder."

Client: Columbia Records, Los Angeles
Art director/designer: Nancy Donald
Photographer: Unknown
Retoucher: Howard Carriker

Manhattan Transfer

Although they look like a rock band in the tinted black-and-white photograph on the flip side of their record album, Manhattan Transfer actually produces an eclectic mix of jazz and swing from the 1930s, '40s and '50s. Art director Sandi Young wanted to capture the style and energy of their music, as well as a period feeling, for Atlantic Records' release of *The Best of Manhattan Transfer*. "Because of budget limitations," she reports, "we couldn't afford both an illustrator and a letterer, but I was able to work with Leslie Cabarga, who does both equally well."

Young wanted a graphic treatment reminiscent of a Cassandre poster. She made a tight layout with a stylized train and New York City landscape to symbolize the group's name and the urban feeling of their sound. Since the upper-third of the jacket must be the most informative, she comped the name in large letters, with "The Best of" to run across the top and then around the border of the entire jacket. "I gave it to Leslie, who has a wonderful design sense for evoking a period, whether its Victorian, '20s, or whatever," says Young. "He refined and improved upon my layout. The '40s train window with the hand toasting the group's name was all his idea and a very pleasant surprise for us. The group loved it."

Young wanted to use a special, more expensive, matte paper "to get the look of an antique poster and pick up the nuances of Leslie's airbrushing." Usually, album covers are printed on glossy board which is cut and assembled. A less expensive way is to use a blank board and wrap the paper around it. That's the method Young employed to stay within budget; she got the quality of paper she wanted for the same overall price.

Client: Atlantic Records, New York City
Art director/designer: Sandi Young
Illustrator/letterer: Leslie Cabarga

Walter Bernard, co-art director on this assignment, felt strongly that an abstraction of the idea of factory automation would work better than a specific image as cover art for a Fortune story on the robotics race. Illustrator Michael Doret was provided with a wealth of photographs for reference. His stylized airbrush painting, reminiscent both in color and line of early 20th-century poster visions of the future, shows man as all-powerful in controlling an array of immense, foreboding machines with the push of a button. But there also is a vulnerability about this tiny fellow that carries a warning. What if he pushes the wrong button? Does he really know which is the right one? Is he confident or frightened? These are some of the questions raised by Doret's statement, and, presumably, by the story it promises.

Doret has arranged his design perfectly to leave space in the top center for the cover story title and for two other cover lines on both right and left—all dropped out of the dark green background in white. The Fortune logo for this issue of February 21, 1983, is in red letters on yellow color blocks to blend with the purple, red, and yellow of the automated monsters.

Margery Peters, who served as art director and designer with Bernard, says the art had to be re-shot because "some of the very subtle air brushing came out as blotches." She also reports that key staff reaction to the painting itself was favorable, "but some thought the cover could have been more reportorial."

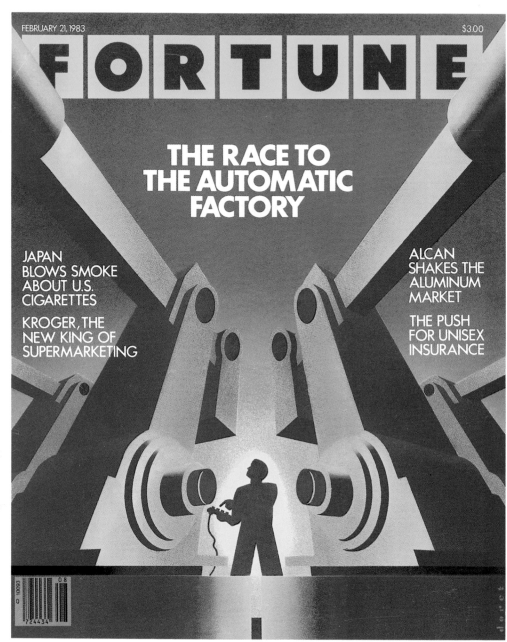

Publisher: Time Inc., New York City
Art directors/designers: Walter Bernard, Margery Peters
Illustrator: Michael Doret

The title of this modern novel by Japan's foremost woman writer refers to the mysteriously evocative masks worn by actors playing women in Nō drama. The protagonist in Fumiko Enchi's book is a frustrated, bitter woman who wears a mask of serenity as she manipulates the lives of others with increasing boldness and cruelty. For this reason, and because the novel is enriched by allusions to Nō plays, Knopf's art director, Lidia Ferrara, decided to use on the cover a striking color photograph of a 15th-century Nō mask of a weeping woman. The Sekai Bunka photo would be shown large on both the front and back of the jacket.

Designer Carin Goldberg presented several comps with different type treatments, the nod going to a design employing Gill Sans Bold Extra Condensed in solid caps. By virtue of its larger first and last letters, the title fits snugly over the top of the mask face. Goldberg had retoucher Ralph Wernli airbrush the title letters with purple, dark at the top and lightening on the way down. The same treatment was used on the smaller spine letters and still smaller letters of the author's name under the front mask. The color, stripped in as separate art, is effective against the cinnamon background and sets off the simple but potent features of the mask.

"Truthfully," says Goldberg, "I preferred another type solution—using Neuland— because it was quirkier and more interesting. I think they chose this because it's easier to read."

Right: Alternate type face (Neuland) submitted by designer.

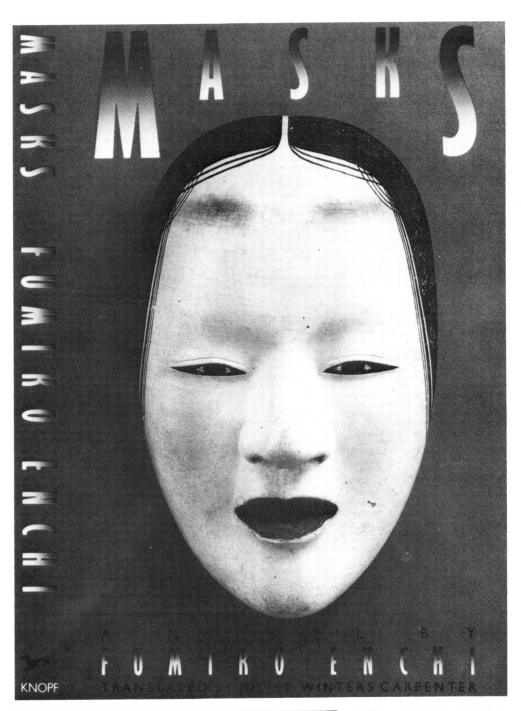

Publisher: Alfred A. Knopf, New York City
Art director: Lidia Ferrara
Designer: Carin Goldberg
Retoucher: Ralph Wernli

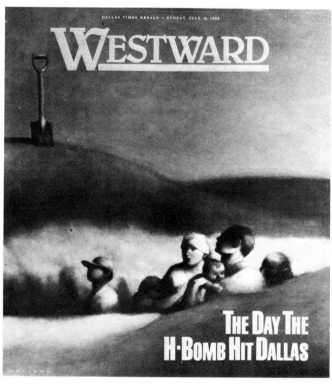

"There's a great throwaway quality to a Sunday newspaper magazine," says Fred Woodward. "People don't keep it around too long, and they don't seem to expect much from it. So I only had to live with my decisions for a week." During his 10 months as art director of Westward, the Sunday magazine of the Dallas Times Herald, Woodward recalls, virtually every cover was produced in about a week. "The finished mechanical went to the printer on Friday night," he says, "and I would have called the illustrator to check availability the previous Thursday or Friday. There rarely was a manuscript, so we thought out ideas on the phone, from cover lines or talks with the editors." Almost never was there time for the illustrator to send pencil sketches. Thus, Woodward first saw art when the finished piece arrived on Friday morning. "I would have ordered at least two varieties of type the night before," he says.

"I did the design on Friday and sent it out that night."

Three weeks later, "for better or worse," the finished magazine came back. "We never saw color proofs, blue lines, anything. Because of this," says Woodward, "I tried to keep everything simple— only one color and just two-screen combinations where possible—to cut down on stripping mistakes and to get better printing." Despite this, the results were erratic, "sometimes good and sometimes bad." But, he concludes, "you couldn't worry about it. I tried to get the illustrators to feel the same way, so none of us would feel too much pressure."

Woodward, who went to Westward in June 1982 (he left to become art director of Texas Monthly the following April), changed the Westward logo because he "didn't feel comfortable" with the underline bar or the swatches which closed up the two "w's." By

Above and top left: Alternate sketches by Brad Holland for "The Day the H-Bomb Hit Dallas" cover.

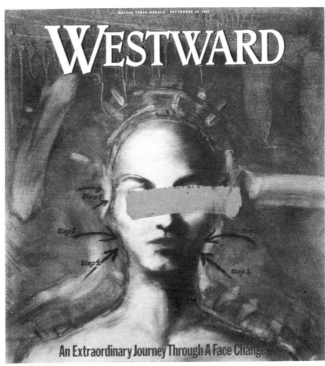

August he had removed the bar under the name and by September had introduced drop-shadowed new lettering, based on old Western posters.

Woodward had a little more time than usual to produce one of his first Westward covers, for a story hypothesizing a nuclear attack on the city of Dallas. "I wanted to start using national illustrators and I thought I'd try to get Brad Holland for this one," he relates, "because the cataclysmic subject matter called for someone with his intelligence and sensitivity." For budgetary reasons, he contracted with Holland for a black-and-white drawing, but after doing some sketches, Holland decided the subject really needed a painting and said he would do one for the same price. "As it turned out," says Woodward, "I was able to get more money."

The painting, a landscape in moody blues, the background totally devoid of any sign that man has been there, focuses on a nuclear family looking out on the desolation from a pit that is a pale slash across the foreground. On an incline above them a shovel is stuck in the ground—was it used to dig the shelter that preserved them? Is it summoning them to dig graves, or to rebuild the world? "Yes, I wondered about the shovel," admits Woodward. Says Holland: "I didn't think about what it meant. If I start to ponder what any particular thing in a painting means, I either exclude it because I can't figure it out or because it then seems I've just dragged it in. I have to forget the narrative and go back to feelings. It seemed to feel right. What it means exactly is for everyone else to decide."

A change of pace was the cover celebrating the anniversary of Frito Lay, the Dallas company that has given the world, as the headline proclaimed, "The Frito: Fifty Years of Munch." José Cruz's

geometic painting in lavender, pink and blue acrylics—with the corner of a Frito's package peeking into the top-right-hand corner—is a New Wave birthday party for the lone Frito sitting on a big lavender dinner plate.

Another of Woodward's Casebook winners was a disturbing cover for a disturbing story about a woman who went in for slight corrective surgery on her jaw and ended up being given a total facelift. The mistake subjected her to loss of identity and made a shambles of her life. Recalls Woodward: "I got a call from the illustrator, Scott Reynolds, saying he had a beautiful pastel drawing of a woman without hair for me (he loves the way people look without hair) and that he was expecting the overnight delivery pickup in 15 minutes. However, he didn't feel he'd really illustrated the loss of identity. He thought he might put a black box over her eyes, but that smacked too much of

those wife-swapping photos. Eventually, with only minutes to go, he did a courageous thing. He just brushed a blue swath across her face." On a murky blue/gray background, the woman's face, that swath of blue almost covering her eyes, emerges from some sort of weird apparatus enclosing her head. Sinister red lines and diagram arrows indicate areas for the surgeon's knife.

In its issue of October 31, 1982, Westward ran a chapter from Simon and Schuster's *Days of Valor: Fighting the Wind*, a book about pioneer women in Kansas. Dagmar Frinta's stylized cover illustration puts a pioneer woman against a flat landscape, barren except for two pigs and a few trees that appear to be blown back by a harsh prairie wind. The woman's high, pointed hair-do bends in the same direction as the trees and she holds a pipe which doesn't quite touch her fingers (a familiar Frinta device). The artist first made a

drawing, then transferred it to sepia blueprint paper, coloring it in muted shades of brown, rose, green and blue with watercolors and Cello-Tak. Were the trees illustrating the wind of the book title? "They could be," says Frinta, "but mostly they were just interesting shapes that echoed the shape of the woman's hair. I put in the pigs because I'd done one on a birthday card for a family member that week and a pig seemed like a good idea."

The cover story for January 16, 1983, was called "Hard Truth: Rufus and the Vietnam Memorial." It was written by a white soldier who didn't know his black friend, Rufus, had been killed until he saw his name on the memorial when it

was unveiled in Washington. In illustrator Vivienne Flesher's pastel illustration the face of a black soldier fills the cover, part of his helmet visible at the top. "Vivienne said she wanted to use just a big face, but she didn't know how to handle the death part," Woodward remembers. "I said, 'Why not just close his eyes? Be ambiguous.' It's softer that way, and I knew that Alan Cober had an illustration inside that was very graphic about death."

Publisher: Westward, Dallas Times Herald
Art director: Fred Woodward
Illustrators: Brad Holland (July 11, 1982), José Cruz (August 22, 1982), Scott Reynolds (September 26, 1982), Dagmar Frinta (October 31, 1982), Vivienne Flesher (January 16, 1983)

The Atlantic

The Casebook jurors applauded the daring of art director Judy Garlan for using a black-and-white photograph on the cover of The Atlantic, a magazine with significant newsstand sales, and the skill with which she did it. "That was a real gutsy thing to do," one juror said. The photo of a boy eating watermelon at a Texas picnic, silhouetted against a cloud-scattered sky, was one of a thousand that Garlan studied in selecting the best representative for a featured photo essay on the 1940s. The photos inside the issue were culled from Nicholas Lemann's about-to-be-published *Out of the Forties* (Texas Monthly Press), based on the 85,000-picture Standard Oil of New Jersey collection housed in the photographic archives of the University of Louisville.

"This picture just jumped out," says Garlan. "Usually there's a sign in a period photo, or a hair-do that tips you off. This said 1940s in a way you couldn't put your finger on. You don't see a kid looking that way anymore. You don't see a sky like that."

Having made her choice from Xerox copies with their high contrast, Garlan was dismayed to discover that the print was gray and washed out. She had increasingly better prints made, then the best of these was retouched to clean it up and get even more contrast. "There were color photos available," reports Garlan, "but I felt that black-and-white better caught the essence of the '40s and the portfolio we were running. The challenge was to create a dramatic cover without compromising the mood." To make the black-and-white quality feel intentional, Garlan actually used five colors. The photograph was printed as a duotone of black and PMS 448 (dark brown) while three muted colors tint the three-part cover line under the logo.

"I also wanted to suggest that the subject was photography," she continues, "and not just the '40s. I didn't want to use a little framed picture, or one with photo album tabs, and space around, so I tried to make the cover itself feel like a photograph as object. Hence, the white border and the raising, through drop shadow, of the logo and other main elements to a plane above the picture."

The issue sold well and appears to have broadened The Atlantic's audience. Best-selling issues, as a rule, had dealt with strong political subjects.

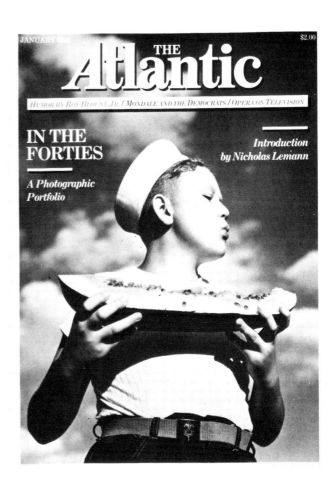

Right: Runner-up to photo chosen for cover.

Publisher: The Atlantic Monthly Co., Boston
Art director/designer: Judy Garlan
Photographer: Esther Bubley/ Standard Oil of N.J. Collection, University of Louisville archives

Flowers&

Since Dugald Stermer had earlier designed the format and logotype of Flowers&, a floral industry trade magazine, he took the liberty of hand-incorporating the name, date and price into the botanical illustration he did for a spring cover. The pencil and watercolor drawing of Spathiphyllum looks like a faded page from the notebook of a 19th-century artist/botanist. This weathered look, achieved with a wash, and classic treatment of botanical illustration make an unusual and effective cover for a publication aimed primarily at a retail trade concerned with bright, modern floral arrangements.

"Since it's not a newsstand magazine," Stermer points out, "I was able to do something that fit my idea of a cover for florists. As far as we can tell, it was favorably received." Flowers& art director Elaine Anderson and editor Barbara Cady liked the illustration so much they asked Stermer to do similar ones to run inside the magazine. For the cover, Stermer's reference was "a plant I bought and drew from life." For the other illustrations of such exotica as the Venus Fly Trap and South Africa's Peacock Morea, he used existing visual materials for reference.

Below: Botanical illustrations commissioned by editors to run inside Flowers& following favorable reaction to Dugald Stermer's cover illustration.

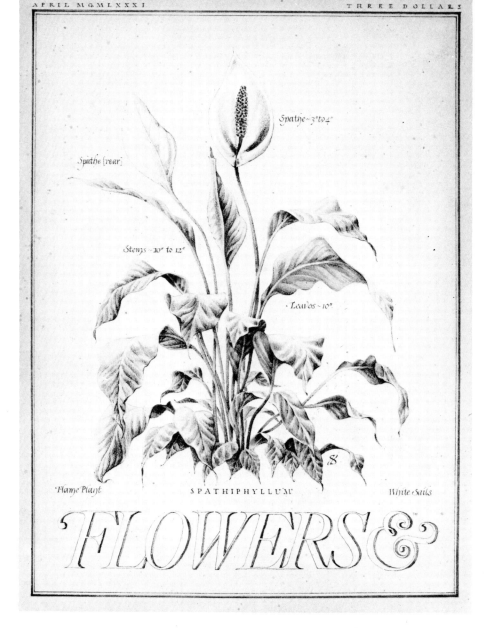

Publisher: Flowers&, Los Angeles
Art directors: Elaine Anderson, Dugald Stermer
Designer/illustrator: Dugald Stermer

Asked by editor Walter Herdeg to design the cover for *Graphis Posters 83,* Seymour Chwast decided he would "do something that doesn't look anything like a poster and is completely different from other poster book covers." The result is a humorous narrative drawing of a burglar tiptoeing out of a bedroom with a framed poster under his arm, totally ignoring a woman lying asleep in the bed. The telltale lighter rectangle on the blue-green wall where the poster had been hanging tips off the viewer as to what's going on.

Chwast is right. Except for areas of flat, posterish colors, his cartoon panel drawing would not be mistaken for a poster. The setting, he says, was inspired by a colored postcard of a motel room, probably from the '50s. Its conglomeration of furniture left over from previous periods is crowned by a gigantic Art Deco dresser with round mirror. Chwast colored his line drawing with a flamboyant array of hues, some of them those edible-looking "Italian ice" shades of raspberry, orange and green.

Publisher: Graphis Press, Zurich, Switzerland; Walter Herdeg, editor
Design firm: Pushpin Lubalin Peckolick, New York City
Designer/illustrator: Seymour Chwast

After success with an extended-play record on its Mercury label by the English rhythm-and-blues group Central Line, Polygram was aiming for a "crossover" with the American release of a second album that had already appeared in Europe. A crossover album is intended to bridge markets, in this case black and pop. Feeling that the English album was geared too specifically to a black audience, Polygram's art director, Bill Levy, and designer Bob Heimall of Bob Heimall, Inc., were looking for graphics that would suggest contemporary music only.

Since the group had taken its name from one of the main London underground train lines, action-packed graphics exploiting this title seemed a natural. The group's picture would go on the flip side. Levy and Heimall decided to try illustrator Montxo Algora on the basis of some greeting cards he had shown them. "They were very interesting, very European," says Levy, "with a musical feeling conveyed by figures of people dancing. We told him, though, we didn't want any figures and nothing trendy."

Algora produced some color concept sketches, "the colors seemed to work," and he was commissioned to do the cover art, an airbrush painting that combines the colors and geometrics of De Stijl with bullet trains speeding in every direction. "We couldn't decide on the type," Levy reports, "so we had Montxo incorporate the title, Central Line, into the painting."

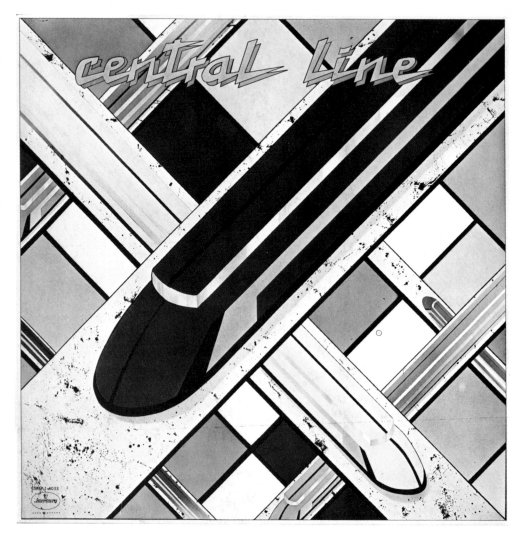

Client: Polygram Records, New York City
Art directors: Bob Heimall, Bill Levy
Designer: Bob Heimall
Illustrator: Montxo Algora

The World's 25
Greatest Marches

The magic words "no sales considerations" were a welcome guideline for Christopher Austopchuk in designing the cover for a CBS Masterworks album of previously released marches recorded by the New York Philharmonic with Leonard Bernstein conducting.

"If you're designing an album for a hot group or performer, one that is expected to be a big seller," Austopchuk points out, "there is a big budget and also a lot of input from a lot of people because there's a lot at stake. If you'll notice, some of the most creative albums are done for small groups, first records by new groups or obscure album titles."

A record like *The World's 25 Greatest Marches*, he explains, has a built-in, but limited, audience. Its members will buy the record whether it's advertised or not, and no amount of advertising will convince someone who isn't interested in marches. The company, of course, plans to make some money, but sales considerations aren't emphasized.

Wanting to find "as nice and humorous a solution" as he could on a low budget, Austopchuk located a black-and-white photograph of a vintage circus poster with an hilarious lithograph of the band and its female trumpet soloist, her filmy dress contrasting with the heavy, much-ornamented uniforms of the male band members. Austopchuk had the photo reshot and hand-tinted to (among other things) give the band gold-trimmed red jackets and to add a pink canopy fringed in turquoise. A dark

blue banner across the top carries the album title in green letters outlined in pink.

Austopchuk says the reaction to the album was favorable, but he doesn't like the way the type turned out. "I was trying something too difficult from a production standpoint," he admits. "There were too many tinted outlines; the type didn't combine well with the artwork and is hard to read."

Client: CBS Records, New York City
Art director/designer: Christopher Austopchuk
Hand colorer: Bob Feldenstein

New York Times Magazine

Since the New York Times Magazine, like all Sunday newspaper supplements, does not compete directly for sales on the newsstands, its art staff can indulge in softer, more ambiguous graphics. The covers may, indeed usually do, make a telling editorial point, but without the hard-sell tactics that are *de rigeur* for publications that must grab the buyer instantly.

One of the covers shown here, for January 30, 1983, refers to a story called "The World of Soviet Psychiatry." In it, Walter Reich recounts the primitive, backward, secretive and regimented aspects of psychiatry in the Soviet Union. Russian psychiatrists, he writes, are not willing to discuss their procedures and storm out of international meetings when they are questioned. There are reports of sinister policies involving the use of psychiatry for revenge or to restrain or immobilize opponents.

"We asked Brad Holland to illustrate this," says art director Ken Kendrick, "because he's so intelligent and we knew he could deal with the political implications in a dignified way. Also, he works fast and we were under the gun." Holland submitted a number of sketches, but his first one, a reference to Swift's *Gulliver's Travels*, was picked. It resulted in a muted painting of a prone man—the patient as Gulliver—staring open-eyed as tiny men climb around on little ladders tying down his head with ropes—the Lilliputians reacting to Gulliver with hostility because he was different from them.

"I'm always uncomfortable with literary references," says Holland. "I feel as though I'm exploiting a cliché." In this case, however, a cliché, if that's what it is, said as much as an entire story.

The choice of a David Hockney fractured photograph for the cover of the March 27, 1983, issue celebrating the Brooklyn Bridge was the fulfillment of a wish long held by

Left: Alternate cover sketch by Brad Holland.

Kendrick, the designer. "I'd always wanted to use one of those Hockney photos, but didn't think the artist would be interested. But when I had a specific idea for a Christmas cover—Hockney-fractured poinsettias—I asked a mutual friend, Henry Geldzahler (former head of cultural affairs for New York City), how to approach him. Henry said to send him a bouquet of poinsettias and suggest the cover. I did and he agreed. But it didn't work out very well and we didn't use the cover."

When the Brooklyn Bridge cover was under discussion, Kendrick again thought of Hockney. "After that other fiasco, I was terribly embarrassed to ask him to do the bridge," Kendrick confesses, "but I did and Hockney said he'd like to, that he had been wanting to photograph the bridge anyway."

"He went to shoot the bridge on one of the coldest days of the year," Kendrick continues. "He used two cameras, one for close-ups and one for distance. He shot loads of color film and had it developed into 4-by-5 prints at a one-hour processing place. Then he made a collage of the prints. He doesn't cut up the photographs—each piece is a full-size print. The collage was so huge when he finished that we just made a chrome and handled it as one photograph."

Hockney's photo collage, the first he had ever done as a commercial editorial assignment, is a distillation of the look and spirit of the venerable bridge. It's all there, in Hockney's instead of the real arrangement—the boardwalk, the wires, the anchorage, bits of landscape from the Brooklyn side. At the bottom we see the tip of Hockney's jeans and shoes as though he's about to set off across the bridge. Similar Hockney collages in the same subdued colors were used in posters and became major symbols of the 1983 centenary.

The New York Times Magazine

MARCH 27, 1983/SECTION 6

The Brooklyn Bridge at its centenary.
A photographic composite by David Hockney.

THE GREAT BRIDGE AND THE AMERICAN IMAGINATION

BY DAVID McCULLOUGH

Publisher: The New York Times Co.
Creative director: Roger Black (January 30, 1983)
Art directors: Ken Kendrick (January 30, 1983); Roger Black (March 27, 1983)
Designers: Ken Kendrick (January 30, 1983; March 27, 1983), Michael Valenti (January 30, 1983)
Illustrator: Brad Holland (January 30, 1983)
Photographer: David Hockney (March 27, 1983)

The Sophisticated Traveler

From time to time the New York Times Magazine carries a Part 2, an adjunct section on a particular topic: fashion, home furnishings, home entertaining, etc. Part 2 for March 13, 1983, titled "The Sophisticated Traveler," inaugurated a new twice-a-year travel section. It carried, among its ads, articles by well-known authors on places guaranteed to arouse the reader's thirst for travel.

Seymour Chwast's commission to design the cover carried the stipulation that it serve as the table of contents billboard. Chwast's solution was a cut-paper design of a stylized traveling couple. The variously shaped and colored stickers on their luggage announce the names of the authors and their travel subject.

The cover expresses in an exemplary way the theme that the sophisticated traveler will know the writers doing pieces on world travel and may even recognize that Chwast is openly tipping his hat to A.M. Cassandre, that master of stylized travel posters.

Above: Promotional poster marking inauguration of new travel section. Illustrator: Michael Doret.

Publisher: The New York Times Co.
Design firm: Pushpin Lubalin Peckolick
Designer/illustrator: Seymour Chwast

The Hollywood
Writers' Wars

"I wanted to evoke the glamor of Hollywood-past and also capture the repressive atmosphere of the time" is the way Fred Marcellino explains the rationale behind his graphically elegant, airbrushed black and brown duotone cover for Knopf's *The Hollywood Writers' Wars.*

To get the gist of the book, you only have to read the five lines of copy Marcellino placed in the lower third of the cover in Bernhard Fashion, a type, he says, that was considered glamorous then—"it still shows up on wedding invitations." The copy reads: "How the formation of the Screen Writers' Guild— and the political passions it aroused among Hollywood's writers, actors, directors and producers in the 1930s and '40s—shattered the closely knit movie community and led to the blacklist years."

Above this, Marcellino slightly angled his hand-lettered title. He wanted the drop-shadowed letters, he says, "to suggest old Hollywood posters and movie titles with their repetitive airbrushing and slightly Fascistic look."

Publisher: Alfred A. Knopf, Inc., New York City
Art director: Lidia Ferrara
Designer/illustrator: Fred Marcellino

Metro

In its two-and-a-half years of existence, Metro magazine lived up to its promise to provide an alternative to what it termed the "slick" city magazines like San Francisco and the Examiner's California Living supplement. Lively, serious, and at times hard-hitting (on politics and social issues), Metro appealed to the audience it had carved out and also won kudos from the design community for the quality of its newsprint graphics, photography, and illustrations.

Depending on ads for revenue, it was distributed free at galleries, art museums, the Civic Center, in the disparate downtown financial and Fillmore districts, and at boutiques and selected stores throughout the city. It carried news of the arts and ran a calendar of events.

The Casebook jurors cast their votes for Metro's 1983 Valentine's Day cover, one of the last published before the financially pressed publication was forced to close. On a Valentine pink background, illustrator Paul Woods combined a cartoon couple with basically realistic figures in flat graphic shapes in the thought balloons. The man's balloon uses symbols and letterforms to suggest game-playing. Her balloon uses different symbols, to show initial uncertainty, indicating that the sexes don't always communicate directly.

"I might have considered photo collage or airbrushing if there had been more time," says Woods, "but since we were rushed, line art seemed best. It would have been nice to have had PMS colors, but we settled for process." All of the color was mechanically separated by using blocking film for each color. The printer did the spreads on the areas without black trap lines. "This process," says art director Vincent Romaniello, "helped us to ensure a good solid coverage and gave us a little more control in getting the exact shade we wanted."

Left: Two alternate cover ideas.

Publisher: Metro magazine, San Francisco; Neal Elkin, editor/publisher
Art director: Vincent Romaniello
Designer/illustrator: Paul Woods

Love: The Art of Romance

Brad Benedict's book of "New" illustrations, dealing playfully, cynically, gladly and sadly with the title theme, was timed to come out for Valentine's Day, but continued to sell briskly throughout the year at Benedict's own Heaven store in Los Angeles and at greeting card shops and some book stores around the country. Benedict, who produced and art-directed the slim, softcover volume for Harmony Books, asked Mike Fink to design the book and Todd Schorr to do the cover. "They wanted something youthful to appeal to the mostly 18-35 age group," says Schorr, "something that would reflect the type of fun, Pop-style art inside the book."

In keeping with initial low-budget requirements for a simple design, Schorr prepared a color sketch based on Fink's idea of a heart-shaped artist's palette with a brush running through it like an arrow. After the publisher suggested introducing a human element, the budget was doubled to accommodate the extra work required for a more complicated piece of art. "The final budget wasn't all that great," says Schorr, "but the job was attractive because of a very leisurely deadline and virtually no creative restrictions other than the initial discussions of concept. We had agreed that only the word 'love' would be incorporated into the painting, with space reserved for title type. This meant I didn't have to worry about working around a lot of letterforms."

Schorr introduced the human element by turning the design into a total front and back cover *trompe l'oeil*. An artist's hands holding the palette and brush appear to be painting a "deliberately corny" oil portrait on canvas of a young couple in love. The word "Love" sits on the painting as though freshly squeezed from a tube of bright red oil paint. The spine of the book becomes the side of the stretched canvas, complete with tacks. The back of the book is the back of the canvas and frame, with charcoal smudges on the canvas and nicks on the wooden stretcher. The illustrator's name is done as one of those imprints burned into the wood by a manufacturer. A love letter sealed with a kiss is tucked behind the canvas.

"For an artist who works exclusively in a sleek, realistic airbrush style," Schorr reports, "it was a difficult challenge—but a real kick—to brush paint the couple's portrait so it looked spontaneous and painterly enough to contrast with the photographic quality of the rest of the cover." The "painting" of the two figures was done in acrylics and the remainder in airbrush using Dr. Martin's dyes and gouache.

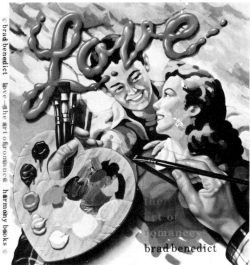

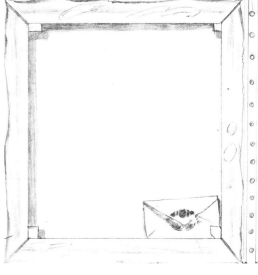

Right: First color sketch with original heart/palette motif. Above: Preliminary sketch of final cover.

Publisher: Harmony Books, New York City
Producer/art director: Brad Benedict
Designer/illustrator/letterer: Todd Schorr

By calling Raw a "graphix" rather than a "comix" magazine, its founders hoped to attract people who appreciate good graphics but don't read comics. Other inducements in the campaign to widen the perception of comics and reach a more literate audience—to make the move from comics-as-kid-culture toward comics-as-artform—include a large format (10½″ by 14½″) and painstakingly careful, some say extravagent, printing on good (70-pound) stock. Last, but not least, the editors and publishers, Art Spiegelman and Françoise Mouly, have looked abroad (mostly in Europe) as well as in the U.S. to find the best in comics art and writing. As one of many surprise elements that keep the publication fresh, Raw changes its cover subtitle for every issue. Issue No.1 was subtitled "The Graphix Magazine of Postponed Suicides"; Issue No.2, "The Graphix Magazine of Damned Intellectuals." Issues 3 and 5, in this Casebook, have equally startling designations.

It's standard practice at Raw to grant cover artists complete freedom. They can work with the suggested subtitle or not, redesign the logo and relocate all cover elements. The two immutables are dimensions and mechanical color separations. Artist/cartoonist Gary Panter was commissioned several months in advance to do Raw 3's cover; the subtitle hadn't been thought up yet. His bizarre single-figure amalgam of five comic-strip characters—Nancy, Popeye, Dick Tracy, Donald Duck and Little Orphan Annie—was deemed too understated to work as a cover.

Mouly and Spiegelman decided to look through Panter's work for a more dynamic image. A striking illustration from his *Okupant X*, a publication of Diana's Bi-Monthly Press, leaped out at them. They knew that this image, a perfect example of the distorted, angry, primitive quality of Panter's art, would work well as a cover. The other

THE GRAPHIX MAGAZINE THAT LOST ITS FAITH IN NIHILISM

Extreme left: Single-figure amalgam of five comic-strip characters was deemed amusing but too static to work as cover. Left: Illustration from Gary Panter's portfolio, previously published as a comic strip, that Raw editors chose for cover.

elements—subtle colors inside the figure, bold color outside, the unobtrusive logo design (as opposed to Raw's own "look at me!" logo)—felt into place at once and the final cover was designed in a day. It fit, too, with the chosen subtitle, "The Graphix Magazine That Lost Its Faith in Nihilism."

Raw selected Ever Meulen (real name Eddie Vermeulen a.k.a. Eddie Filippo), Belgium artist/illustrator, to develop the cover image for Raw 5. He chose to work with the subtitle, "The Graphix Magazine of Abstract Depressionism." He submitted two cover sketches, one in jest (a comic character looking out of the window at a skyful of abstract images) and the one the editors chose. A month later Raw received Meulen's finished line art and tight color sketch—a rich, varied, beautifully integrated, narrative-non narrative mix of abstractions, weird perspectives, landscapes and characters, both human and animal. It looks as though the New Wave just broke and rolled over it, leaving as "debris" on the shore an assortment of exactly drawn and placed images.

The editors were pleased with the design but disturbed by the shrill colors—tangerine orange and lime green, to name two. Meulen wasn't happy with the colors, either, and encouraged Mouly, a former colorist with Marvel comics and an experienced printer, to alter at will. For two frustrating months she experimented, without success. All of the picture components were so carefully worked out that even the minutest color shift upset the perfect, but precarious, design balance. Mouly tried using different palettes for different parts or covering with clear varnish, but nothing worked. Finally, she decided simply to use the original colors in more subdued tones.

Left: Alternate sketch submitted in jest by Ever Meulen as a take-off of subtitle "The Graphix Magazine of Abstract Depressionism."

Publisher: Raw Books & Graphics, New York City
Designers: Françoise Mouly, Art Spiegelman (No. 3); Ever Meulen (No. 5)
Illustrators: Gary Panter (No. 3); Ever Meulen (No. 5)
Color separations: Françoise Mouly

Martin Briley

Martin Briley had been in the music business for close to 10 years, with a following as an instrumentalist and back-up singer—but mainly as a song-writer—before he decided to put a band together, achieving enough success before long to encourage Polygram to issue an album of his songs. Briley, involved in the cover design from the beginning, wanted to base the art on an album song title, "Fear of the Unknown."

"We knew that title would call for fantasy or surrealism," recalls Bill Levy, Polygram's art director. "In looking through Norman Walker's portfolio we saw that he had done very realistic things, but there were indications he could handle a surrealistic subject." Briley, Levy, Walker and Bob Heimall of Bob Heimall, Inc.—long associated with Polygram as a designer—"sat around," says Levy, "and talked and talked and talked" over concepts until they hit on the solution. They decided early on to use Briley's trademark beret and red boots. Then they sought an image to express fear of the unknown that everyone could identify with. Briley related how terrified he was in childhood when he was sent to the principal's office to report a misdeed, standing in the open door with a beam of light shining in his face and seeing only a big shadow inside.

"Then we talked about a lonely room," Levy continues, "and I suggested an open empty window casting the shadow of a man on the wall and floor. 'Great,' they said. Now we had to figure out how to get Briley on the album. 'Put him in a painting on the wall,' someone (I don't remember who) said. 'Fine,' we all said, 'case closed.'"

Walker's acrylic painting— "with apologies to Magritte," says Levy—evokes the album's title to perfection. The curtains blow in an empty window whose shadow across the room is joined by that of a man with legs extending along the floor until they disappear into Briley's

red boots. Briley, in a red beret in the painting over the fireplace, is the little boy standing in the doorway. Levy says this design is one of his personal favorites and the album itself, although it wasn't a big seller, was well received critically and had a big enough audience for Polygram to do a second Briley album.

Since Briley was working on the West Coast at the time, the recording was made there and the graphics handled by Lumel/ Whiteman designers of Los Angeles. They hired Stan Watts to illustrate Briley's cover song title, "One Night With a Stranger." Watts did an acrylic painting in murky, purplish blues of an undistinguished motel room with a picture on the TV screen and a photo of Briley in white beret on the wall. A woman in sexy black lingerie sits smoking on the bed while a man struggles upward— as though through water—to get out of the room, which has turned into a pool whose surface is the ceiling. On the flip side is a photograph of Briley in shirt, tie, jacket and dark beret in a swimming pool, looking as though he had just shot up out of the motel room and one night with a stranger.

The same large sans-serif type is used for the artist's name on both albums. It was intended as a logotype for Briley to unite these albums and a third being planned.

Right: Back of One Night with a Stranger *album.*

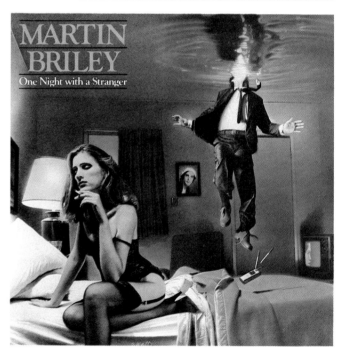

Client: Polygram Records, New York City
Art directors: Bill Levy, Bob Heimall ("Fear"); Murray Whiteman ("One Night")
Designers: Bob Heimall ("Fear"); Murray Whiteman ("One Night")
Illustrators: Norman Walker ("Fear"); Stan Watts ("One Night")
Photographer: Murray Whiteman ("One NIght")

Look at Me

"The previous illustration for the jacket had just been rejected," relates art director Louise Fili of Pantheon Books, "when Judy Pedersen walked in with her portfolio, with exactly the sense of what I was looking for." Fili is referring to the jacket for British author Anita Brookner's second novel, *Look at Me*, and she was seeking cover art that would express "in a quietly beautiful and thoughtful way" the tone of a story about a lonely woman librarian who is given a promise of love and companionship, only to have it disappear and plunge her back into loneliness. Brookner's tale of hope and disappointment is introspective and slow-moving. Fili wanted a cover that would subtly project the mood of the story and found it in Pedersen's soft pastel of a woman sitting in a lonely room, staring pensively off to the side. The image on that side of the drawing is daringly close-cropped. The woman's face is strong and interesting, but the light, warm apricot, rose, ivory and gray of the pastels convey the delicacy and sensitivity that were so crucial to the cover's success.

"The response was very positive," reports Fili. "It worked well in bookstore display. This is another case of my pleasure in assigning an illustrator a first book jacket. I like to use artists who have worked in other disciplines, but haven't done jackets, because they have a fresh approach." She adds, "In this instance, Judy Pedersen also came through very quickly in order to meet a preliminary deadline."

Publisher: Pantheon Books, New York City
Art director/designer/type designer: Louise Fili
Illustrator: Judy Pedersen

Chicago Flash

Since this was only the second issue of a glossy new graphic arts magazine directed at advertising agencies and design studios in Chicago and throughout the Midwest, designer/illustrator Don Cosgrove aimed for a cover "which would make an audience like that want to look inside."

Publisher Paul Casper had specified only a singular, strong graphic image, leaving the subject matter and concept up to Cosgrove. The singular image, with, Cosgrove says, a surreal twist, is a window-washer whose first swipe across the dirty windows that gray out the urban cityscape produces a rainbow of clean, bright colors. The contrast of the curved linear line of the shadowed man's figure and the mechanical straight lines of the window frame set up a tension and balance that play against the arc of paint colors announcing that spring has arrived (this is the April issue). Green from the color swipe is picked up in the window-washer's sun glasses and blue in his shirt.

Cosgrove submitted several thumbnail sketches and agreed with Casper on the solution. Cosgrove then did a pencil drawing, followed by a gouache painting with a black line overlay. "The whole job was a pleasure," he says, "especially seeing it printed on really excellent cover stock and laminated. It was also fun because our studio is on the 43rd floor and ever since we moved here I've been fascinated by high-rise window-washers, but never had a chance before to share that fascination."

Left: Thumbnail sketch.

Publisher: Chicago Talent, Inc.
Design firm: Cosgrove-Duggan, Chicago
Art directors: Paul Casper/Chicago Flash; Dan Cosgrove
Designer/illustrator: Dan Cosgrove

Long Beach Blues Festival

Young designers often volunteer to design a poster for no fee in return for the experience and the chance to have their work recognized. Such a "freebie" was the handsome poster Tom Antista designed in 1982 for the blues festival sponsored each year by radio station FM88 in collaboration with California State University at Long Beach.

Working up his comp with Color-Aid papers of mostly brilliant blue, Antista outlined the shape of a guitar in turquoise, a panel of curved solid color in the lower left of the poster that becomes a single line profiling the opposite side of the instrument. The hole in the guitar—done as a triangle—and the title on the upper left are a deep lavender. The upper side of the triangle is bordered with one narrow strip each of turquoise and a yellow that is picked up in information type at the bottom. The diagonal placement of the silver strings completes the geometric design.

Casebook jurors were impressed by the "total excellence" of the work—the image, type treatment and beautiful, silkscreened satin finish. Antista says he learned the silkscreen technique during an internship at the in-house Graphic Communications design studio which McRay Magleby heads at Utah's Brigham Young University. "Just the right amount" of gloss base is mixed with dull inks to give a satin, rather than a matte, finish. A different mixture was used for the shiny silver strings, overprinted last.

As it turned out, after an immediate enthusiastic reaction to Antista's solution and a go-ahead, the festival's organizers decided at the last minute they would rather have a harmonica image. Could he change it? No, replied Antista, not at that late date. He printed the poster anyway and it is in a number of galleries in Southern California.

Client/designer/illustrator: Tom Antista, Playa Del Rey, CA
Printer: Carawan Printing
Colors: Cobalt blue, turquoise, lavender, yellow, silver
Size: 17¾" by 26½"

Goodwill Opens Doors

After Goodwill Industries of Dallas went to Cunningham and Walsh with $1500 intended for the design, production, printing and distribution of its 1982 annual report, the agency knew that an unusual solution was called for. They found it by designing a poster with the financials on the back.

First, C&W assembled a group of printers, typesetters, paper houses and separators willing to donate their services. It then fell to VP/creative director Alan Lidji, who quarterbacked the project, to design something simple and economical, but striking enough for everyone involved to use as promotion. A poster seemed the logical answer.

Using the concept "Goodwill Opens Doors," Lidji designed the room of a house with two walls cut away, a bright blue sky with white clouds showing through the open door and a large arched window. Bright yellow sunlight streams in at the door and across the floor. Lidji cut Color Aid papers in intense shades to make his comp. The room, in three shades of gray, floats on a bright red background. A shiny ¾″ grid in the red background was accomplished by dropping it out when dull varnish was applied. The sky and clouds, printed in three-color process, came from a photo Lidji found in the portfolio of his photographer-wife, Laynie.

Printed offset litho in five additional colors on Monarch 100-pound Karma white cover, the posters were distributed in tubes to participants at Goodwill's annual meeting. The response was so good that Lidji decided to continue the concept for future reports, using other illustrators or photographers.

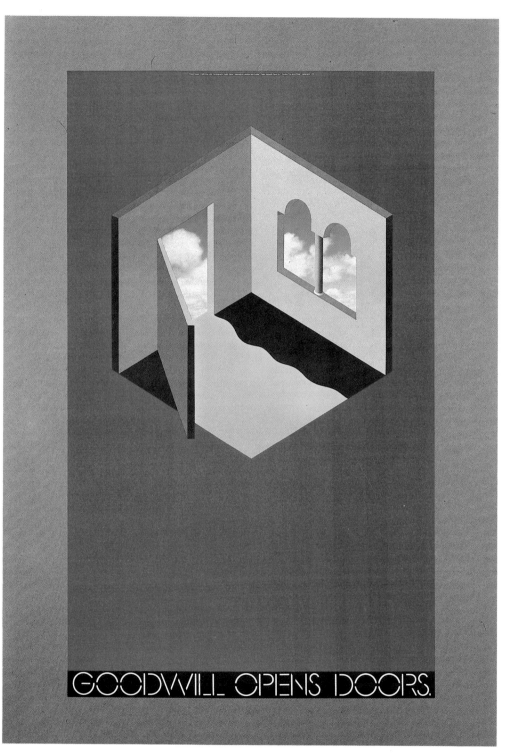

GOODWILL OPENS DOORS.

Client: Goodwill Industries of Dallas
Agency/design firm: Cunningham and Walsh, Dallas
Art director/designer/illustrator: Alan Lidji
Printer: The Jarvis Press
Typography: Jaggers Chiles & Stovall
Color separations: Martinez & Rutter
Colors: Red, three grays, yellow, three-color process (clouds) plus dull varnish
Size: 21½″ by 35½″

De Stijl

As it often does with local cultural events, Dayton's Department Stores of Minneapolis planned a tie-in with the Walker Art Center's large-scale exhibition of works from the De Stijl art movement that existed from 1917 to 1931. In addition to ads, a major promotional item was an in-store poster featuring Gerrit Rietveld's so-called red/blue chair, which had become the symbol of the Walker's show of some 250 paintings, drawings, architectural models, reconstructions of interiors, and furniture by artists of the Holland-centered international movement. A reproduction of the Rietveld chair was on display in the store.

Art director/designer Karen Brown knew she would use the chair as well as the rectangles and squares of bold primary colors—red, yellow, blue—and the black, gray and white that characterized the De Stijl artists as they sought to create a universal style in painting, architecture and design. But she also wanted to blur the De Stijl hard edge, to give it something of the tentative-primitive look she had admired in the work of an illustrator she had seen reproduced in an Italian magazine. She placed the chair alone in a room bare except for a few De Stijlish geometric shapes floating on the walls. "I thought the bare room personified that spare, and to me, isolated look of De Stijl. But then I wanted to soften the whole look, to bring it into the '80s with a lighter quality."

With only three weeks available, Brown lacked time to track down the European illustrator. So she called in Joe Sellers, a "super-realistic" airbrush artist she had often worked with and explained what she wanted. They both felt the painting Sellers turned in was a bit stiff and lacked life. Brown suggested he take it back and make it "messier" by rubbing it in places with gray and white pastels. "After Joe finished," says Brown, "I made a few more squiggles here and there

with colored pencil." Brown placed the lettering in a typical De Stijl corner angle, but "decorated" the letters with color and softened the background panel with shadow panels. All of these additions give an ethereal quality totally at odds with De Stijl methods and cause the viewer to do a double-take.

Client: Dayton's 700 on the Mall, Minneapolis
Art director/designer: Karen Brown
Illustrators: Karen Brown, Joe Sellers
Copywriter: Lisa Dolinger
Printer: Colormaster Press
Color: Four-color process
Size: 22″ by 28″

A seasonal challenge to designers is to find new ways to say Merry Christmas and Happy New Year. Amazingly, every year brings a crop—not a big one, to be sure—of marvelous and fresh visual solutions to this recurring problem.

The Casebook jurors were enthusiastic about one of these felicitous Christmas designs, a small poster submitted by the Hill graphic design group of Houston. The poster simply shows 14 views of a pepper turning from green to red. A green pepper is centered near the top; then, in four rows of three images each, we see the pepper ripening in shades of red and green until the final image is a red pepper, centered near the bottom. "Merry Christmas" in small type at the top and "Happy New Year" at the bottom over the company's logo and name, in even smaller type, is all there is. One juror, in the ultimate tribute, exclaimed, "Why didn't I think of that?"

It really is the same pepper, too. Photographer Jim Sims set up the pepper on a white background in his studio and shot it every day or so over a two- to three-week period. The peppers in the individual slides were stripped and all arranged at the same angle. In the separations, the four-color shadows were dropped out and a softer black screen shadow substituted to give a floating look.

Client: Hill/A Graphic Design Group, Houston, TX
Art director: Chris Hill
Designers: Chris Hill, Joe Rattan
Photographer: Jim Sims
Printer: The Olivet Group
Colors: Four-color process
Size: 9⅜" by 24¼"

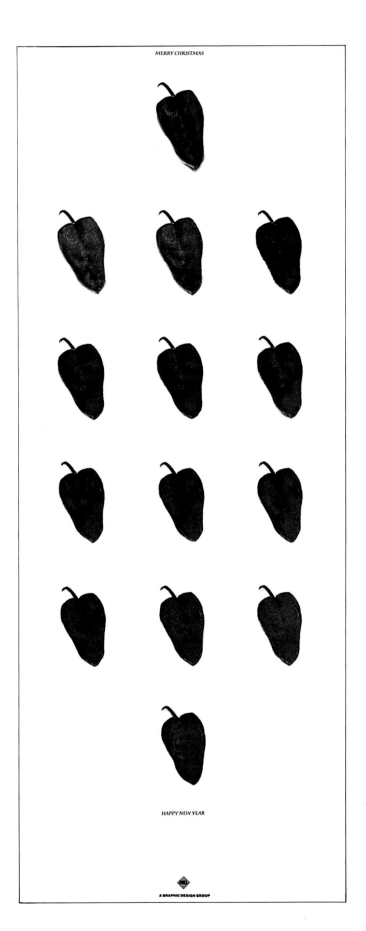

Saul Bass: Update

When Saul Bass accepted an invitation to address the Los Angeles Art Directors Club at the Biltmore Hotel in March, 1983, he also volunteered to design a poster for the occasion. Taking the form of a handwritten signature, the poster demonstrates the elegantly simple, idiosyncratic style of the veteran graphic designer and filmmaker.

At the top is the quintessential tool of his trade—a fresh yellow pencil. In the center, the pencil writes "Saul" and then snakes itself into "Bass"; under that, a pencil stub with pink eraser intact. One line of small type at the bottom gives place, time, etc.

The poster was lithographed three-color process separation both as 500 posters and 2000 to-be-folded mailers. Even the mailers ended up on walls, and the L.A. Art Directors Club had its largest turnout ever.

Client: Art Directors Club of Los Angeles
Design firm: Saul Bass/Herb Yager and Associates, Los Angeles
Designer: Saul Bass
Colors: Red, yellow, pink, black
Size: 22″ by 28″

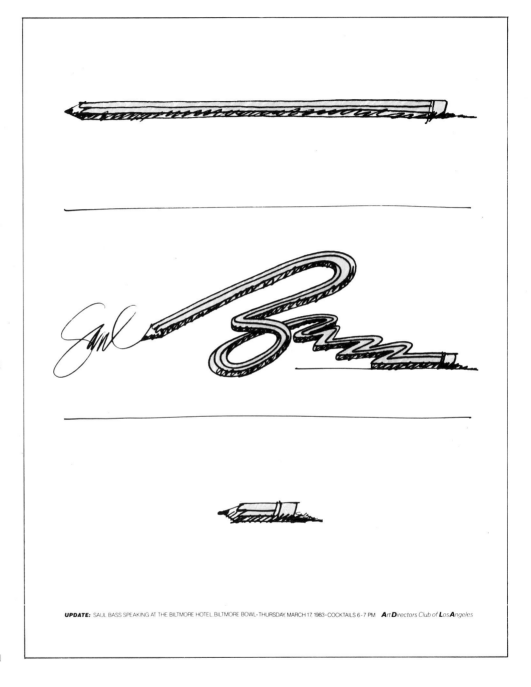

UPDATE: SAUL BASS SPEAKING AT THE BILTMORE HOTEL, BILTMORE BOWL · THURSDAY, MARCH 17, 1983 · COCKTAILS 6 - 7 PM   Art Directors Club of Los Angeles

For Christmas 1982, designer Milton Glaser sent his friends a colored drawing of Monet which he had had stone-lithographed in Paris. One of the recipients showed the lithograph to Gerald van der Kemp, director of the Monet museum at the artist's home in Giverny, France, who thought the image would make a wonderful commemorative poster for the museum, and asked Glaser to design one. Glaser sent a copy of the 12″ by 14″ lithograph and a sketch showing how it would appear on the poster. The idea was accepted and the posters, measuring 24″ by 36″, were printed offset litho in four-color.

Glaser drew the original in crayon and pencil on textured pastel paper, working from photographs of the artist. In a line or two for each, Glaser has given us a touching catalog of Monet trademarks—the broadbrimmed hat, the cigarette clamped in his mouth so that it extends over the beard, the pocket handkerchief. But more of a trademark are the colors. The deep, textured shadowing under the hat that obscures the top of the face gives the impression that the entire image, on its pale yellow background, is suffused in sunlight that reflects off the bright, light tints of blue, yellow, rose and red that might be paints on a palette, or might even be water lilies. Glaser called the drawing "Monet's Palette," a play on words that could mean only the colors Monet used, or could refer to those clumps of color in the foreground.

The title MONET is in 3½″-high Futura Light, white dropped out of a light brown border. Monet's dates, 1840-1926, and Giverny appear at the bottom in a smaller version of the same type treatment.

Client: Musée de Claude Monet, Giverny, France
Designer/illustrator: Milton Glaser
Colors: Four-color
Size: 24″ by 36″

The American Book Awards

The paintings Brad Holland did for the American Book Awards ceremony of 1982 were involved in a game of musical chairs before ending up in their permanent places on the poster, the cover of the program book, and as an illustration within the program.

"I intended the first painting as the poster," says Holland, "but they used it for the cover of the program." This was a square acrylic in shades of blue and gray that was wrapped around the vertical (4"-by-9¼"), stiff-covered program book. An urban landscape made of different sizes and shapes of books, half of this art (the back cover of the book) was used on the ticket to the ceremony, the other half on the invitation to an after-ceremony reception. "The second painting," says Holland, "I meant for the cover of the book, but they thought it was too ironic, and put it inside." This is the figure of a man, also in blues, with a book for a head. The book is placed horizontally and is slightly open, so it looks as though it is talking.

"Now we still needed a poster," recalls Holland. "I had sent them a bunch of sketches, and I went back through these with Harlan Quist, who was putting it all together. We settled on an image I did a few years ago for a book review. Those people had wanted changes I didn't choose to make, so I took it back." The reddish-brown poster image, the one chosen by the Casebook jurors, shows a man wearing one of those Brad Holland 19th-century long fitted suit coats and opening a door which is the front cover of a book. He faces a vista of green grass and a blue sky with pink clouds—book as door to life.

A limited number of posters were signed and given to TABA contributors and supporters. The rest were sold.

Right: This Brad Holland painting was used as a wrap-around cover for the American Book Awards program book and also appeared on the tickets. The front cover illustrated the reception ticket, the back cover the ceremony ticket. Far right: An alternate rough sketch.

Client: The American Book Awards, New York City
Art director: Harlan Quist
Type designer: Ken Diamond/The Art Patrol
Illustrator: Brad Holland
Printer: Princeton Polychrome Press
Colors: PMS blue, brown, green, pink
Size: 24" by 36"

CEREMONY

The Third Annual Presentation of
THE AMERICAN BOOK AWARDS
*Tuesday, April 27, 1982
at 4:00 p.m.
Carnegie Hall
Fifty-Seventh Street at Seventh Avenue,
New York City.*

Admission by this ticket only.

RECEPTION
*following
the Third Annual Presentation of*
THE AMERICAN BOOK AWARDS

*Tuesday, April 27, 1982
from seven to nine p.m.
Sheraton Centre / Imperial Ballroom
Seventh Avenue at Fifty-Second Street,
New York City.*

Admission by this ticket only.

Three times a year, for many years, McRay Magleby has produced inventive, appropriate, eye-catching solutions to what could be a pretty dull assignment even the first time around—posters urging students at Brighman Young University to register in time for the fall, spring and summer semesters and thus avoid a late fee. Besides the repetitive nature of this assignment, tight budget, time and size restrictions apply to all of the work that BYU's in-house Graphic Communications Studio does for the various university departments. But Magleby, who heads the studio and teaches graphics at BYU, feels the restrictions are more than offset by the challenges involved and by the freedom he's given to pursue his own ideas.

Registration posters for the 1982 spring term illustrate the usual limitations encountered by Graphic Communications, which Magleby runs with the help of six professional designers and the part-time efforts of a crew of students. The time schedule was two weeks from start to finish, the budget $425 per poster for a run of 150 each, and the size limited to the approximate 20″ by 27″ maximum allowed on campus bulletin boards. On the other hand, the client approved the concept over the telephone and liked the first solution presented.

Recognizing the intrinsic appeal of vintage aircraft, Magleby used World War I fighter planes as his motif. Choosing three planes with markedly different designs, and using photos and diagrams, he made pen-and-ink drawings—complete for the side view and of one-half of the plane for front and bottom views. He made a film positive of each half and statted it, then flopped the positive to get a stat of the other half. These were trimmed with an X-acto knife and fitted together on Magleby's light table.

On the posters, the three views are arranged under the names of the planes in Garamond caps across the top, with copy at the bottom relating the plane to the registration deadline, i.e., "Don't be shot down by the $10 late fee." As usual, the posters were designed for silkscreen printing with large, flat areas of solid colors which overlapped, where possible, to achieve a third color. Generally, eight colors resulted from five runs of five colors in specially mixed inks on Karma cover.

This registration poster series was the most popular so far, Magleby reports, inspiring him to design World War II planes for the following summer semester.

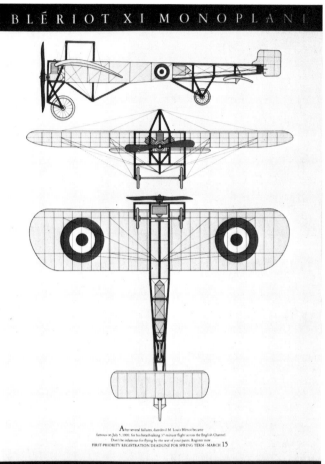

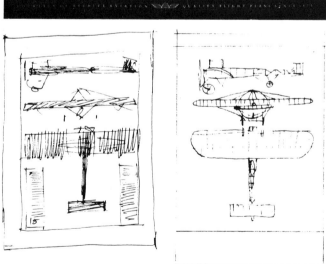

Fokker DR-1 Triplane   **Sopwith F. 1 Camel**

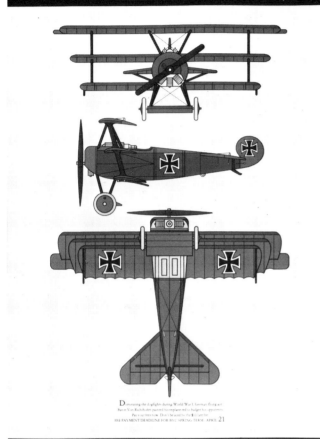

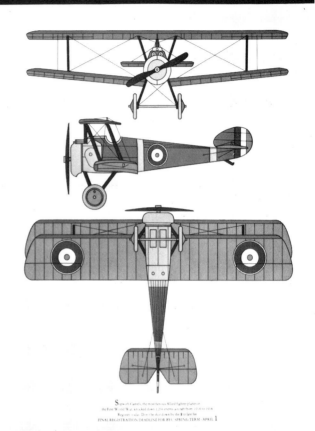

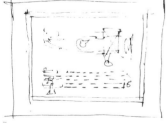

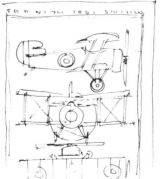

Opposite page below and this page left:
Thumbnail sketches of various aircraft.

Client: Registration Dept., Brigham
Young University, Provo, UT
Design firm: Graphic Communications,
Provo, UT
Art director/designer: McRay
Magleby
Copywriter: Norman A. Darais
Printer: Rob Carawan, Provo, UT
Colors: Green, blue, red, silver, black,
brown, gray (Sopwith); red, blue, brown,
tan, silver, black (Blériot); red, black,
silver, brown, black (Fokker)
Size: 19½″ by 28″

National Bickford
Foremost Collectibles

After the photo-engraving firm of National Bickford merged with Foremost printers a few years ago, the new company published a series of promotional posters themed to winning combinations—ham and eggs, Tinkers-to-Evers-to-Chance, etc.—in an effort to convince potential customers that National Bickford Foremost was itself just such a winning combination.

The company's strategy was to become known as a designer's printer. Their audience, therefore, was made up of art directors, designers, company presidents, etc.—people who not only recognized quality color separations and printing but were in decision-making positions.

Following the success of the first series, the client asked its designer, Tyler Smith, to prepare a second phase of mailers on a three-a-year schedule. The only stipulations were that the series be interesting and emphasize striking separations and fine printing. It was decided to feature collectibles—things like dolls, rugs, stamps, automobiles. These items, in fact, became the subject of the first four posters, all selected by the Casebook jurors.

"A series like this," says Smith, "has to be more than beautiful photographs and printing. There must be an intriguing concept that can go on for a while. The copy in this series was important; it had to tell an interesting, informative story and tie the concept together."

The posters, at 20½″ by 37½″, are large enough to make a promotional impact and stop short of presenting display problems. Three use outsize color photographs—an oriental rug, a vintage Mercedes roadster, and a collection of antique dolls. The fourth presents the U.S. Jenny stamp, valuable because it was printed

upside down, actual-size on an 18½″-by-28″ matte black background.

"I photographed the Jenny stamp myself," says Smith. "I'm an amateur collector. Mine is just the ordinary one printed after the mistake was discovered. We turned it around so it became a 'collectible' for the poster."

Client: National Bickford Foremost, Providence, RI
Art director/designer: Tyler Smith
Copywriters: Geoff Currier, Gail Welch
Photographers: Myron Taplin (rug); Kurt Stier (dolls); Clint Clemens (car); Tyler Smith (stamp)
Colors: Four-color process, PMS gray plus varnish; matte black (stamp)
Size: 20½″ by 37½″

California Design

For its California Graphic Design exhibition, the AIGA needed a poster which would solicit entries from designers throughout the state and also announce the event to the public. It was important to distinguish the AIGA show from other, national exhibitions for a California audience. Of the six proposed sketches featuring California images, designer Kit Hinrichs feels the chosen solution best symbolizes the entire state, "not only its design aspects, but also its cultural, geographical, architectural and climatic character as well."

The poster, a horizontal close-up photo by Terry Heffernan of the front of a navy-blue 1947 Ford "woody wagon," includes these California elements in reflections on the bumper, grille and fenders—Northern California on the right, Southern California on the left. The method of achieving the reflections had not been clearly defined in the original conception. But it had to be inexpensive, since there was no budget; all of the people and firms were volunteering their services. "Since we couldn't afford extensive retouching, costly dye transfers and dupe assemblies," Hinrichs points out, "we needed a single, uncomplicated piece of art for reproduction. We opted for the uniqueness of a photo." To get both the Northern (Golden Gate, San Francisco skyline) and Southern (palm trees, Los Angeles) California reflections, a special set was built around the car with a 180° silhouette. A series of color strobes simulated sunset. No retrouching was needed on the finished chrome and production costs were kept under $500.

The project encountered a number of lucky and unlucky breaks. Lucky was the discovery of a legal "vanity" auto license plate belonging to a Los Angeles graphic designer which obligingly read "California" in small letters over a large-lettered "DESIGN." Unlucky was the weather. Owners of the kind of mint-

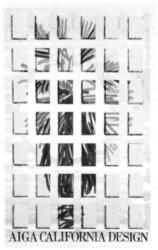

condition "show" car required for the shooting will not drive them if it is raining or even looks like rain. "After four consecutive weekends of rain and a fifth one predicted," says Hinrichs, "panic was setting in as the deadline approached. Then, designer Gene Icardi produced, 'rain or shine,' this gorgeous car that gave us not only bumper reflections but the unexpected fender and grille reflections which ultimately made the shot."

With a call for entries on the back, the poster drew more than 2500 entries and several thousand people attended simultaneous openings in San Francisco, Los Angeles and New York.

Above: Three alternate designs. It was felt that the design selected for poster (top) best symbolized the entire state of California.

Client: American Institute of Graphic Arts, New York City
Design firm: Jonson Pedersen Hinrichs & Shakery, San Francisco
Art director/designer/copywriter: Kit Hinrichs
Photographer: Terry Heffernan/Light Language
Printer: Anderson Lithography, Los Angeles
Colors: Four-color process
Size: 36½" by 17"

Life and Death

The annual collaboration between Manhattan's School of Visual Arts and the Master Eagle Family of Companies in the presentation and promotion of an exhibit of student work continues to benefit the school, the students and the well-known graphic arts firm. Each year, students of the Media Arts Department, co-chaired by Richard Wilde and Marshall Arisman, are given a theme to illustrate. The competition is juried by a faculty committee, which also chooses the work that will be used in a poster/mailer to the professional community and potential students and two invitations to the show at the Master Eagle Gallery, one for SVA students and one for Master Eagle's friends and customers.

The theme for the 1983 exhibit was "A Matter of Life and Death." Students were asked to create a two-part visual statement to communicate the concept, admittedly a touchy subject, but one that would stretch the students, testing their taste as well as their imagination and execution.

One hundred entries were picked for the show, actually 200 pieces because of the two-part stipulation. Chosen for the poster were Paul Yalowitz' two colored pencil drawings of a jaunty door-to-door hairbrush salesman who picks the wrong door—that of a bald man who does him in, then stands over the body clutching a hairbrush and appearing to ask, "Well, can you blame me?" The muted colors—lavender, rose, blue, gray, brown and green—are treated to resemble rough stone or plaster board. This, along with the bullet head and tiny slit eyes of the hulking attacker, creates the kind of foreboding and menace engendered by the characters in a Harold Pinter play.

Viewing the non-verbal sequence as a kind of very early silent movie, Susan Spivack and Bill Kobasz of the School of Visual Arts Press designed a nostalgic title panel across the top of the horizontal

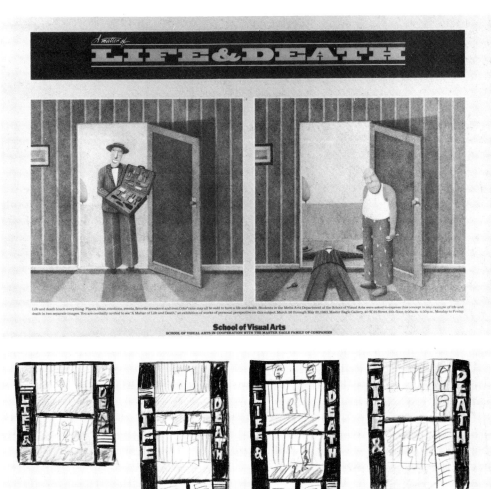

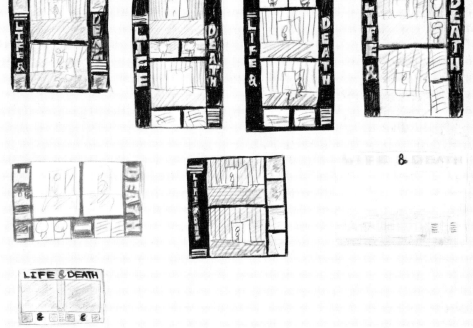

poster's two drawings, almost as another illustration. On the long black panel they combined brush lettering by John Rea with a turn-of-the-century woodcut type, hand lettering in places (to create an ampersand, for example), dropped out over a lavender strip textured in colored pencil by the illustrator.

Above: Series of layout sketches. All were discarded in favor of simpler design with title panel (top).

Clients: School of Visual Arts; Master Eagle Family of Cos., New York City
Art director: Richard Wilde
Designers: Susan Spivack, Bill Kobasz
Illustrator: Paul Yalowitz
Brush lettering: John Rea
Copywriter: Pam Manser
Printer: Master Eagle
Colors: Four-color process
Size: 33″ by 23″

Reaganism

For its fifth biennial show in the winter of 1983, the board of the Lahti, Finland, international poster competition changed its rules on subject matter. Instead of assigning a theme, as it had in the past (National Health, for instance), the competition board told entrants to create their own theme; "get whatever we wanted to off our chests" is the way designer Lanny Sommese puts it. Sommese, whose Casebook winner titled "Reaganism" was included in the 1983 Lahti show, is a long-time participant in the Finnish biennial.

At the time the entry invitation arrived, Sommese says, he was "down" on some of President Reagan's ideas and chose those feelings as his theme. Designed as a parody of a 19th-century circus flyer, the poster utilizes a linoleum-cut image Sommese had done for a limited edition of protest poetry. By adding hand-lettered typography with the rough-hewn, shadowed look of the old-time flyers, Sommese had his poster.

The image, a fiendish-looking Uncle Sam whose reflection in the mirror is a ferocious animal that reaches out and bites him on the nose, exudes the energy and insouciance that are Sommese trademarks. He confesses that when he was cutting the linoleum ("I'm not very good at it") his knife kept slipping and gouging the surface, so "rather than start over, I just gouged it a lot more to make the slips look intentional."

When the 8″ by 10″ lino cut was photo-enlarged to size, it produced a rough quality, which is just what Sommese wanted.

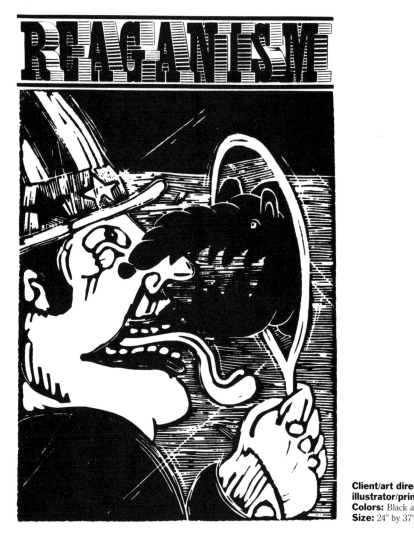

Since economics dictated silkscreening, and the printing would be done with the help of apprentice design students (Sommese is head of graphic design at Pennsylvania State University), a rough style would "make mistakes less evident." Also, because of the "less than perfect" silkscreen production, Sommese limited himself to two colors—black with typography in rusty red—on tan Hammermill cover stock. The 24″ by 37″ size is "the largest standard sheet of paper readily available in State College, Pennsylvania."

In view of the political nature of the poster, Sommese told his students they could refuse to help if they were opposed. None refused.

Client/art director/designer/ illustrator/printer: Lanny Sommese
Colors: Black and red
Size: 24″ by 37″

Right: Companion poster entry showing Uncle Sam rolling the tiny form of a man back and forth on his tongue "like a cat playing with a mouse."

Beaux Arts
Halloween

The Beaux Arts Ball at Pennsylvania State University has a long tradition among architecture and fine arts students. It has become tradition, too, for Lanny Sommese, head of graphic design at the University's School of Visual Arts, to design the poster announcing the annual Halloween event. These posters have become collectibles for students, faculty and graphic designers.

The image in the Beaux Arts Halloween poster chosen by the Casebook jurors looks as though it has just climbed down from a medieval cathedral. A two-faced monstrosity with little animals pushing out of the eyes, mouths and noses, it imparts a deliciously creepy-crawly Halloween ambience.

With only the usual one week from initial contact to printed piece, Sommese made an 8″ by 10″ drawing on tracing paper with Pentel pen, then photo-enlarged it to a Kodalith positive which he continued to work on until "we made the stencil and printed it." Since the 60 posters would be silkscreened as part of his student apprentice design program, Sommese, as usual, kept the image rough to cover up any production problems. Also, as usual, colors were limited, this time to red and green on tan Hammermill Cover. Sommese felt the serif type treatment (Century School Book dropped out of the green top and bottom borders) was appropriate to the overall look. The T-square tucked under the monster's arm was added later "to give the religious look of a cross, the religion being architecture and design."

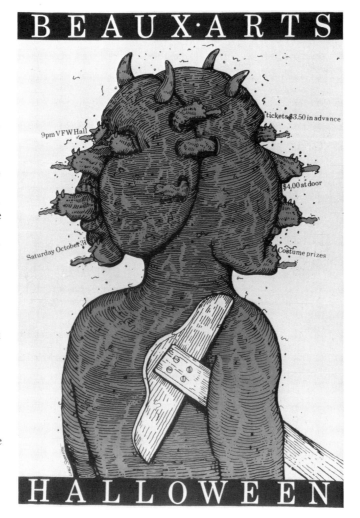

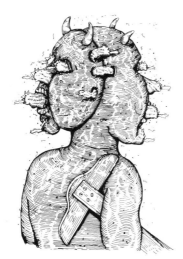

Left: Original pen-and-ink drawing.

Client: Dept. of Architecture/School of Visual Arts, Pennsylvania State University, State College, PA
Art director/illustrator: Lanny Sommese
Designers: Lanny Sommese, Peter Salter
Printer: Penn State Design Practicum
Colors: Red and green
Size: 24″ by 37″

During the first seven years that it conducted its arts apprenticeship program, New York City's Department of Cultural Affairs collected an array of information that would be valuable to aspiring writers and artists if it could be made available in a practical way. In 1981, it was decided to put it all together in a writer's source book, and Henry Geldzahler, then head of the department, enlisted the aid of professionals to help.

Seymour Chwast answered the call for cover art, which was done in two colors, black on yellow, to minimize costs. The book, detailing information about grants and funding, volunteer lawyers, writers organizations and many other services, was so successful that the department published a revised edition in 1983, along with a companion source book for artists, also with a cover by Chwast.

Chwast redid his cover for the writer's book, adding color, and the new illustration was used for 7000 posters intended to promote the book and, through their sale, to raise funds for the department. Chwast combined the ideas of New York and writers into one image, a Chrysler Building drawn as an old-fashioned pump fountain pen with its point soaring up to become the skyscraper's tower. The Chwastian cars and people streaming around the bottom were added to "give it scale." Chwast redrew his original line drawing and added color with Cello-Tak. The nicely placed serif type chosen by Toshi Ide (as Grey Advertising's contribution) makes clear that the subject is serious despite the lighthearted drawing.

Right: Seymour Chwast also did the cover for a companion source book for artists.

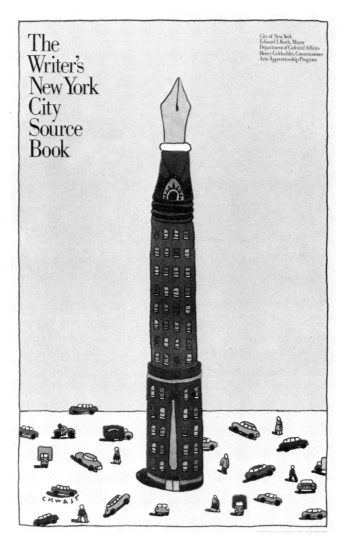

Client: Department of Cultural Affairs, City of New York
Agency: Grey Advertising
Design firm: Pushpin, Lubalin, Peckolick
Art director: Toshi Ide
Designer/illustrator: Seymour Chwast
Printer: Collier Graphic Services
Colors: Four-color process
Size: 25½″ by 39¾″

1812 Overture
Solennelle

A traditional fund-raiser for the Dallas Symphony Orchestra League is a dinner-dance celebrating the orchestra, with civic-minded members of the community pitching in to help make the event a success. The contribution of Richards, Sullivan, Brock & Associates was to design and prepare the mechanical for a poster invitation.

Art director/designer Brian Boyd's solution was a page of (violin) music from Tchaikovsky's *1812 Overture* which starts out straight at the top of the poster, but then, not quite half way down, explodes into a shower of celebration images and colors. The staff lines disintegrate into streamers and the musical notes become confetti. Invitation copy at the bottom asks for a reply *allegretto*. "I picked the *1812 Overture*," says Boyd, "because it's familiar and because all of the cannons going off are like a Fourth of July celebration."

The design went right from thumbnail, which the client "loved," to mechanical. So the League could turn out an attractive poster at minimum cost, Boyd chose inexpensive beige stock (Mohawk Vellum) and a two-color press, using split fountain to maximize color. Printing the 22⅛″ by 34¾″ posters sideways allowed the color of the music to change from dark blue for the conventional format at the top through lavender, pink turquoise and yellow as it breaks up into antic, New-Wavey bits and pieces.

Left: Thumbnail sketch of poster idea.

Client: Dallas Symphony Orchestra League, Dallas
Design firm: Richards, Sullivan, Brock & Associates, Dallas
Art director/designer: Brian Boyd
Copywriter: Mark Perkins
Printer: Heritage Press
Colors: Gray (type), split-fount blue, pink, tourquoise, yellow
Size: 22⅛″ by 34¾″

A New Face

The assignment to design a self-promotion poster for a New York typehouse was an unusual one for artist Barbara Nessim, who generally is responsible for the illustration rather than total design. The typehouse, Scarlet Letters, owned by red-haired Julie Brumlik, wanted to feature a major offering of new typefaces. "I knew initially that I didn't want it to look like a type reference poster, but that's about all, except," adds Nessim, "that I planned to use hand-lettering and blow it up, leaving the new faces, in actual size, as the only type. It was rather daunting, though, because there were more than 200 faces and I'd never worked with that much type before."

Her first designs, with titles like "New Faces: There are thousands of faces in town, and now we have every one of them," used drawings of four women's faces, set diagonally and framed by columns of typefaces. Then Nessim decided on the simpler treatment the client chose. She began, as she often does, to look back through her sketchbooks (she does about four a year) for ideas. The face of a woman she had done in pencil in 1978 seemed appropriate. She redrew the face in pen-and-ink and tinted the drawing delicately with pale shades of blue, green, rose and mauve watercolors. The face was then blown up large and flanked by columns of type on the left and right. The words "Scarlet Letters" curve away from the woman's neck like a scarf. A desert landscape (a Nessim trademark), done in a few lines at the bottom, gives a feeling of distance. Stylized spikes of hair, a flying twist of earring and the company telephone number in large figures at the bottom are antique gold, like the narrow band at the top. Now, the title reads: "A New Face Communicates."

There were so many requests for posters that the initial run of 15,000 was soon depleted and another 15,000 were printed.

Extreme left: Alternate layout idea.
Left: Original drawing from artist's sketch book.

Client: Scarlet Letters, New York City
Designer/illustrator/letterer: Barbara Nessim
Art directors: Barbara Nessim, Mare Early
Printer: Sterling Roman Press
Colors: Four-color plus gold
Size: 22″ by 34″

Nocturnal Prowler

Designers at the Smithsonian Institution's National Zoo in Washington spend a lot of time doing "scientific work," that is, graphics involving exact replicas of zoo inhabitants, correct in all the minutia of feathers on a wing or whiskers on a face. "That's why a series like this is a little reward for the designer," says Robert Mulcahy, head of the zoo's office of graphics and exhibitions, referring to an ongoing series of abstract posters aimed at increasing public awareness of the special nature of the world's endangered big cats.

The series poster picked for inclusion in this Casebook depicts the fluid motion of the tiger as an animated assemblage of colored forms—a shoulder, a foreleg, a head, etc. "That's how it began," Mulcahy recalls. "I said, why don't we cut out abstract forms of parts of a tiger's body and see how they move?" Using notebook brads, he made joints so that various movements could be simulated in a homemade, animal version of a "draw me" manikin. Then, designer Ramona Hutko refined the geometrics of the shapes on grid paper, statting these and making drawings. She added color as the drawings progressed.

The poster was silkscreened in 14 colors, including black background—the night through which two tigers are stalking. Done during "downtime" between other assignments, it was allowed 30 days from design to production. Making so many precise overlays, Mulcahy says, was "time-consuming but worth the effort." The perspective was abstracted, too, and that makes some colors appear to be printed over others, but each color—muted shades of blue, green, orange, rose and yellow—represents a separate run.

Five hundred copies of the poster were printed on L.O.E. cover. It can be seen at Smithsonian museums, as well as at other museums and various zoos around the country.

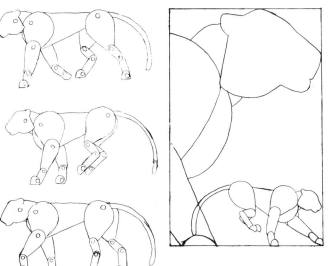

Left: Two of many line drawings by designer Ramona Hutko indicating progression from "manikin" shapes to finished design (top).

Client: National Zoological Park, Smithsonian Institution, Washington, DC
Design firm: Office of Graphics and Exhibits, National Zoological Park
Art director: Robert E. Mulcahy
Designer/type designer/copywriter: Ramona Hutko
Printer: Jay Schlueter/Office of Graphics and Exhibits
Colors: 14 silkscreen
Size: 20″ by 30″

Holland America Cruises

A massive program to reposition Holland America lines vis-á-vis its competition as the cruise line of old-fashioned luxury included the commissioning of five oil paintings by Wilson McLean to be used as posters but presented as signed fine art. "We looked back through the company's archives," reports Noreen Young, director of creative services for the century-old line. "We unearthed some really glamorous graphics from the glamorous period of ocean travel when liners were used as transportation from point A to point B. We wanted to capture the feeling of some of those graphics, like Cassandre's, but bring them into the 1980s when ships are used merely for pleasure cruises. We wanted to project the emotional appeal of a cruise."

Young and Keith Bright of Bright & Associates had liked some previous illustrations of McLean's for Holland America and he was chosen for the poster series. Actually, his paintings skip back past the period of the '30s and late '20s, with its highly stylized, abstracted steamship and rail posters, to an earlier time when fantasy was confined to background and foreground, or surrounding graphics, and the ships themselves were rendered faithfully—back to, for example, Frederick Charles Herrick's Royal Mail posters. Each of McLean's stylized landscapes contains, besides a ship in the distance, a huge fantasy element typical of the five cruise areas. In the Casebook-selected poster, "To Alaska with Holland America," an enormous silvery salmon swims in the sky in front of an organically detailed glacier of the Inland Passage from Vancouver to Glacier Bay. The

Holland America to Alaska   Wilson McLean

Client: Holland America, Seattle
Design firm: Bright & Associates, Los Angeles
Printer: Jeffries Lithograph Co.
ALASKA CRUISE:
Art directors: Keith Bright; Noreen Young/Holland America
Illustrator: Wilson McLean
Colors: Four-color process
Size: 16″ by 21″ mounted to 22″-by-28″ 80-pound cover

ship in this poster is very slightly distorted, more so than any others in the series. Fantasy element for the Trans (formerly Panama) Canal is a huge butterfly, for Bermuda an outsize shell and shore bird.

For a different Holland America promotion—commemorating the SS Rotterdam's 25th (silver) cruise around the world—Charles White III's silkscreened poster moves a decade or two further along the nostalgia trail, but with originality and panache. The extent of abstraction owes a lot to Cassandre *et al*, but the treatment is pure 1980s airbrush. White's silvery ship and undulating wake, seen as an aerial view, are so abstract, he says, that it takes a moment to realize what you are looking at. Once over that hurdle, however, the poster's festive mood personifies a high-ticket ocean cruise. It seems to say, "Take every penny of your savings, if you have to, and come with me!" Anything round like a funnel is turned into a pearl and the shower of pastel New Wave streamers and confetti (cut from Chromo Tech and pressed on) move up as smoke from an invisible stack rather than down as gravity would have it. As it turned out, the poster was never used for the silver cruise, but, says Young, the artwork will appear on myriad shipboard items such as menus, postcards, luggage stickers, etc.

SILVER CRUISE:
Agency: Chiat/Day, Inc., New York City
Art directors: Bob Dion/Chiat Day; Keith Bright
Designers: Charles White III, Paul Mussa/Willardson White Studio
Illustrator: Charles White III
Colors: Four-color process plus two match colors and silver silkscreened
Size: 24" by 36"

Left: Two posters by Wilson McLean — Trans (formerly Panama) Canal and Caribbean—in same cruise series as Casebook winner.

Hot Seat

It is hard to imagine a more appropriate poster-invitation than one that Woody Pirtle designed for Knoll International. The furniture designer/manufacturer was inviting its friends in the Dallas area to a Sunday afternoon chili cook-off. The sole image on Pirtle's large (24″ by 36″) poster, titled "Hot Seat," is a laid-back, upholstered office chair in the form of a red chili pepper. Typical of the playful touches Pirtle often injects into his designs, one of the "chair's" casters has fallen off and it looks as though springs are poking out of the upholstery.

Pirtle made his drawing with a grease pencil to get the soft, fuzzy look which adds to the fantasy. Spare, sans-serif lettering in red, a white background and solid, bright yellow foreground project the company's reputation for clean, simple but imaginative design.

One thousand posters were silk-screened on heavy stock and the ones that remain have already become collector's items. Other Casebook jurors agreed with one who said it was a "perfect solution to the problem."

Client: Knoll International, New York City
Design firm: Pirtle Design, Dallas
Designer/illustrator: Woody Pirtle
Printer: Lem Ramsey
Colors: Red, green, yellow, black
Size: 24″ by 36″

Tango

To attract a young, "upbeat" audience, the owner of a new Dallas nightclub called Tango asked Pirtle Design for a poster he could use as an invitation to the opening and as a commemorative to sell at the club later. Presented with several roughs of ideas, the client selected one with bright, colorful figures on a night-clubby black background. That description, however, doesn't do justice to David Kampa's antic, abstract dancers or to Mike Schroeder's lettering.

Art director Woody Pirtle considered 24″ by 36″ to be the minimum size for the design to be effective. For the illustration, Kampa cut figures out of brilliantly colored paper, geometric approximations of people—hands, feet and faces are just jagged slashes—in various positions of the tango. These, he arranged in rows of dancing figures. Since four-color process was going to be used, it was decided to add texture to the 12 dancing "couples" to make them more interesting, because, while none of the figures was exactly the same, they were similar. Kampa textured a few figures with colored pencils, but mostly he scraped shavings from the pencils onto the figures with a knife. He pushed some of the waxy shavings around with a roller; others, he rubbed with tissue.

The resulting, vividly colored figures capture the intense, high-energy level of a 16,000-square-foot nightclub with all the accouterments of disco—loud music, flashing lights and multi-media effects. You can almost hear a tango melody as the little dancers swoop through their motions. The letters in the title seem to dance, too. Schroeder says he started with Times Roman Bold and replaced the serifs with smaller ones from Times Roman Regular. But once the letters were turned on their sides, he didn't like the overall proportions so he redrew most of them.

Client: Tango, Dallas
Design firm: Pirtle Design, Dallas
Art director/designer: Woody Pirtle
Designer/illustrator: David Kampa
Type designer: Mike Schroeder
Printer: Heritage Press
Colors: Four-color process
Size: 24″ by 36″

Founded 20 years ago by a group of young volunteers, the Children's Theatre Company has become an important part of life for both adults and children in the Twin Cities of Minneapolis and St. Paul, winning national and international acclaim for the vitality and imagination of its performances. Now a permanent company of actors, technicians and administrators with its own school, Children's is unique for having on its staff an artist who does all of its major graphics, has upon occasion designed sets and costumes, and has composed original musical scores for 30 productions.

Since 1970, Stephen Rydberg has created a large body of posters and other artwork which gives the company an inventory it can use for promotional pieces and for items to sell in its gift shop. One of the two posters chosen by the Casebook jurors— "Pipes of Pan"—was done for the 1981-82 season; the other— "Red Poppies"—for 1982-83. The illustrations were both created in acrylic on canvas, a medium Rydberg was using at the time.

Rydberg says that "Pipes of Pan," in dark greens, blues and reds, refers to that season's musical productions. More than anything, it is reminiscent of the fine illustrations in oils that enhanced books during the first half of the century, before they went the way of leather bindings and other publishing amenities. "Red Poppies" has a flat, oriental look. The vase of flowers and pulled-back curtain, Rydberg says, are a recurring motif of his. The flowers could

The Children's Theatre Company and School   81-1982
Minneapolis   USA

Red Poppies

be in a window, symbolizing the theater as a window to the world. On the other hand, it could be a theater curtain with the vase of flowers representing the performance.

The posters are approximately 22″ by 29″ and the artist painted to size. No preliminary approaches exist: "I just attack the canvas," he says. The posters were sent as premiums to seasonal (September-June) ticket-holders and the art was used on the covers of season brochures.

Client: The Children's Theater Co. and School, Minneapolis
Designer/illustrator: Stephen Rydberg
Printer: Bolger Publications
Colors: Four-color process
Size: 22″ by 29″ (1981-82); 22¼″ by 29¾″ (1982-83)

The CHILDREN'S THEATRE COMPANY and SCHOOL
82 - 1983   MINNEAPOLIS, USA

Tulip Time

The area in and around Holland, Michigan, was settled generations ago by immigrants from the Netherlands. Each year, the residents of Holland celebrate their Dutch-American heritage with "Tulip Time," a four-day festival of costumed *klompen* (wooden shoe) dances, street scrubbing, house and windmill tours, the partaking of such Dutch culinary specialties as *saucijenbroodjes* (pigs in a blanket), and—most important—tulip viewing. Eight miles of tulips line Holland's streets and millions of others are planted in commercial gardens. Not so many when compared to the billions of bulbs grown in the original Holland, but still one of the largest displays in the U.S.

The festival is organized and run by a non-profit corporation of volunteers who call on people in the half-dozen or so towns that make up "Dutch Country" to donate money or services. One of these towns is Zeeland, headquarters of Herman Miller, the furniture designer and manufacturer. When some members of the festival organization became aware of the poster tradition at the New Orleans Jazz Festival, they asked Stephen Frykholm, Herman Miller's corporate art director, to design a poster to celebrate and generate revenues for the 1982 Michigan event. They were familiar with Frykholm's colorful, glossy posters announcing the annual Herman Miller summer picnic. Originally intended only for distribution in Herman Miller offices and facilities, most of these big (25″ by 39½″) screen-printed posters with large, flat areas of specially mixed-to-match colors are now sold to defray production costs, so in addition to the recognition they have received in the U.S. and abroad, many adorn office and residence walls in the Zeeland-Holland area. Picnic food items are blown up so large the images become voluptuous abstract patterns in which recognizable elements—strawberries in a fruit bowl, for instance—take on overwhelming importance.

"I like big posters," says Frykholm, "so I decided to use the 'picnic' treatment here and feature tulips, a rather obvious choice." With Herman Miller donating his time, Frykholm designed immense red tulips on a pink background for the 1982 poster. Sales were so successful that he used the same horizontal format in 1983 for a bunch of huge yellow tulips seen bee's-eye view from the top.

"I sketch with the camera," says Frykholm, who takes rolls of 35mm film, gets quick prints from a "shopping mall photo developer," and traces shapes he likes ("drawing is not my forte," he admits), perhaps combining, in this case flower, images from a number of prints into one design. This is enlarged and a full-scale line drawing made, showing line weights. Frykholm then indicates color to his printer ("I may just cut a hunk out of a piece of fabric") who mixes Cudner & O'Connor lacquer inks to match.

Client: Tulip Time Festival, Inc., Holland, MI
Design firm: Herman Miller, Zeeland, MI
Art director/designer/illustrator/type designer: Stephen Frykholm
Letterer: Pam Van Dyken
Printer: Continental Identification Product
Colors: Two reds, two greens, pink, lavender (1982); two yellows, two greens, two blues, two blacks (1983)
Size: 39½″ by 25″

The Swimmer

Michael Schwab originally executed his powerful image "The Swimmer" as a full-color newspaper ad for an airline. That's why the lines are so simple and the colors so bold. However, it was rejected by the client as too intimidating for its targeted audience. So Schwab turned it into a promotion poster for himself and for a local San Francisco printer, Mastercraft Press.

One can understand the airline's reluctance. Influenced, as Schwab readily admits, by those strong, slightly threatening, German travel and propaganda posters of the '30s and early '40s, it might scare off an American traveler of today. "I'm impressed by the German posterists of that period," says Schwab. "I've done a number of things in that style."

The swimmer in the poster chosen by the Casebook jurors is not your weekend sunbathing beauty, even though she holds a multi-colored beach ball. Looming strong and confident, akimbo arms bursting through the black border of a vivid (specially mixed) yellow background panel, this woman is at least a champion swimmer and probably from the look of the swimming pool behind her, an Olympic champ. Solid black shading on her face and body enhance the vitality of the image on the panel standing out from a glossy white border.

Schwab works from black-and-white Polaroids which he takes in his studio, using actors as models whenever possible. He often has the models dress in white to get more interesting shadows. The color comes later, when he's drawing. "I actually design the image with the models," he says. "The drama comes from the lighting and the bodily attitude of the models. That's why I like actors as models, because they can give me what I have in mind. I do the fine-tuning at the drawing table."

Above left: Black-and-white photo of model by artist Michael Schwab from which poster drawing was made. Below right: Other poster by artist in the same earlier 20th-century German style.

MICHAEL SCHWAB
ILLUSTRATION/GRAPHIC DESIGN

Clients: Michael Schwab Design; Mastercraft Press, San Francisco
Art director/designer/illustrator: Michael Schwab
Printer: Mastercraft Press
Colors: Seven PMS colors, specially mixed yellow plus varnish
Size: 18″ by 33″

Color from Harper House

Richards, Sullivan, Brock & Associates were delighted when Harper House, a local Dallas company specializing in four-color separations and engraving, asked them to design a poster showing off Harper House's work. Because the assignment was an offbeat one for their portfolio, RSB&A agreed to absorb all design and mechanical time, plus miscellaneous expenses other than typography and printing, in return for complete freedom in creating a unique poster.

Early on, art directors Brian Boyd and Ron Sullivan decided on two things: they wanted to use a diamond format and they wanted to take this opportunity to hire illustrator José Cruz, whose work they had admired for some time but whose style, they felt, wasn't suited to, say, their annual reports. "José was a fresh, new talent on the local scene, with a wonderful eye for color," says Boyd. "He does geometrics, combinations of real flat color, very strong and full of energy."

Cruz, working in acrylic with both brush and airbrush, aptly demonstrated the abilities of Harper House with a Pop-geometric illustration which shows a youngster sipping a soft drink and eating popcorn while watching a movie through multiple 4-D glasses, each lens a square of one process color. The four colors extend in rays, changing as they spread out over other colors. The soft-drink carton, popcorn box and background geometrics are equally colorful.

Positioning the square illustration as a diamond on the square white background formed other diamonds within

the illustration and made a frame of still other diamonds. Along one diagonal, designer Boyd placed five lines of copy, the initial colored letters spelling out "Color" and the rest of the letters gray. Each line of copy refers to color, i.e., "Roses are red. Sometimes." The much larger letters of Harper, in tinted varnish, fit between each copy line. Taking their intended back seat to the

color, the pale gray of the type and especially the letters in varnish are subtle, to say the least, and barely show in camera reproduction. Boyd says these subtleties were possible because the audience, 70 per cent in the Dallas-Fort Worth market, were familiar with Harper House.

Client: Harper House, Dallas
Design firm: Richards, Sullivan, Brock & Associates, Dallas
Art directors: Brian Boyd, Ron Sullivan
Designer: Brian Boyd
Illustrator: José Cruz
Copywriter: Larry Sons
Printer: Broadway Printing Co.
Colors: Four-color process and gray, plus two varnishes
Size: 24″ by 24″

Sweeney Todd

Bill Nelson, self-described as a frustrated actor who is too scared to get on a stage, has kept close to the legitimate theater for years by designing program covers and promotion pieces for friends who run the Barksdale Theater in Hanover Tavern, Virginia. In the fall of 1982 he volunteered to do his first poster for the theater, one that would promote a production of Stephen Sondheim's musical, *Sweeney Todd,* and also be offered for sale at the theater as a souvenir.

"I had the show leads photographed in their costumes and worked from black-and-white photos," says Nelson. "I was after a dynamic, dramatic image which, with bold type, would be instantly read and remembered." He achieved this with a painting that is like a camera stop-action of the climactic first act curtain scene in which Sweeney Todd and Mrs. Lovett raise high the tools of their trade—the razor with which he does in his victims and the rolling pin she uses for baking them into meat pies.

Nelson airbrushed the background green shading to rose at the bottom. He painted the figures first in muted shades of dark red, rose and green watercolors, then went over them with Prisma colored pencil. A friend, Ann Northington, did the title in Magic Marker on a paper towel. "I thought red blood would be too cheap a shot," says Nelson. "Since I wanted to use green in the poster, orange seemed the best choice." He adds, "My only regret is that I spelled Sondheim's first name wrong. However, he liked the poster anyway."

Client: Barksdale Theater, Hanover Tavern, VA
Designer/illustrator: Bill Nelson
Letterer: Ann Northington
Printer: Spencer Printing
Colors: Four-color process
Size: 17" by 26"

The W.O.R.K.S
Silk Screen Design

A growing market for more expensive, so-called "high end" posters, has led to an increase in companies that publish and distribute them. The publishers are commissioned, mostly by small businesses, to produce fine art posters that can be used as promotion as well as sold in galleries, museum shops and better poster stores. The publishers provide art direction, design, illustration, whatever, then print the posters and arrange for their distribution to the right market.

Such a publisher, Drucker, Vincent of San Francisco, hired Tom Kamifuji to do a series of illustrations with an oriental motif. One of these was used in a dramatic poster for the W.O.R.K.S. silkscreen house, which, of course, did the printing. A colorful open fan, set against a black background, hugs the top of the 24″-by-36″ poster. The bottom two-thirds is blank except for the long burnt orange and orange tassle hanging down from the narrow, shiny gold frame of the fan.

After doing his drawing, Kamifuji made the composition to size with Zipatone. The green, blues, fuchsia, lavender, yellow, orange and burnt orange of the fan and the background are printed matte, emphasizing the gloss of the gold frame. Fluorescent paint was mixed with the inks to make the colors glow. The W.O.R.K.S. name, in letters which Kamifuji devised by spacing out Futura Light and rounding off the corners, was printed in the tenth run on fine, black Arches paper. Kamifuji says the fan doesn't conform to any traditional oriental style—"I just made it up."

Client: Drucker, Vincent, Inc., San Francisco
Art directors: Tom Kamifuji, Alan Drucker, June Vincent
Designer/illustrator/letterer: Tom Kamifuji
Printer: The W.O.R.K.S.
Colors: Nine silkscreen
Size: 24″ by 36″

ITC Fat Face

When a St. Louis type house approached David Bartels to design a series of posters promoting its services, the only limitations were budget (small) and time (one month start to finish on each poster). Budget considerations dictated the use of existing art where possible. Otherwise, except for the wording of the promotional copy for Master Typographers, Bartels was given free rein.

The poster for ITC Fat Face was one of seven in the first phase of the ongoing project. Artist Roy Carruthers had done the illustration for the cover of a novel that remained unpublished. Incredibly appropriate to the title, the horizontally elongated face appears to be a police rogue's-gallery photograph of a big thug wearing a shoulder holster whose ludicrously narrow straps and tiny gun create a feeling of unease by their very oddity. The device of geometric lines measuring the face, labelled with meaningless letters and numbers, could be the work of a mad phrenologist. Bartels says the illustration has just the quality of imaginative realism he wanted for a series meant to be decorative and informative.

Green was airbrushed on to give a shading of color to the top of the title's white letters dropped out of black. Different complementary colors were used this way throughout the series.

Twenty-five-hundred copies of each poster were printed four-color litho on Ikonolux Gloss. Bartels reports that many have been framed for permanent display by companies and individuals.

Right: Two other posters in series, for Marvin and Revue typefaces.

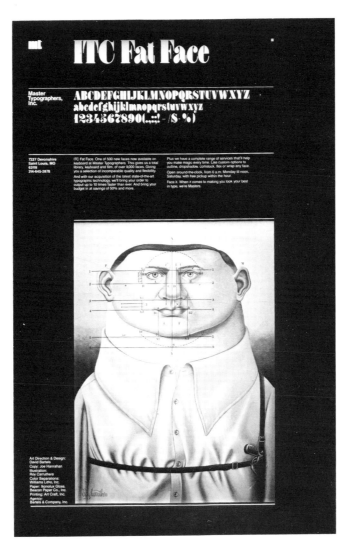

Client: Master Typographers, Inc., St. Louis
Design firm: David Bartels & Co., St. Louis
Art director/designer: David Bartels
Illustrator: Roy Carruthers
Copywriter: Joe Hanrahan
Printer: Art Craft, Inc.
Colors: Four-color process plus dull varnish
Size: 14″ by 22″

James Joyce Symposium

"The things of Joyce I've read," says McRay Magleby, "seemed very abstract and to alter reality to the way he perceived it." So it was fitting, when designing a poster announcing the James Joyce Symposium at Brigham Young University, for Magleby to alter Joyce's face by abstracting it. Each of three roughs he submitted on behalf of BYU's Graphic Communications Studio was progressively more abstract than its predecessor, and the client chose the third, most altered, version. The client in this case was the Department of Humanities, which, with four other departments, was sponsoring a two-day series of lectures, papers, and panel discussions on Joyce, along with readings from his works.

After approval, Magleby made a pencil drawing on tissue of the face—all angles relieved by startling, vacant, round eyeglasses. He then redrew the sketch over standard grid paper, making his angles conform to the grid. Although not his original intention, the finished drawing looks like a computer print-out, linking, Magleby now feels, the first "watershed" author of the 20th century to another of the century's influential developments, one that revolutionized technology.

Using BYU's traditional silkscreen printing (with split screen blends this time) and the size decreed by campus bulletin boards, the poster more than fulfills another requirement that Magleby and his staff of professional and student designers always face: posters must fight to put across their message amidst typical bulletin board clutter. Framed in red on a black background, easily carrying an enormous amount of type (information on the symposium) dropped out in silver gray, the Joyce image leaps out at the viewer. The eyeglass lenses and several geometric elements glisten in the glossy white of the Mead Mark I coated stock against matte-finished red, gray and flesh tones.

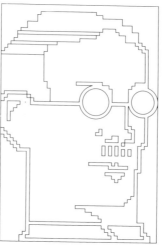

Extreme left: Preliminary rough drawing. Left: Later sketch, redrawn over grid paper.

Client: Dept. of Humanities, Brigham Young University, Provo, UT
Art director/designer/illustrator: McRay Magleby
Printer: Rob Carawan, Provo, UT
Colors: Hand-mixed red, black, flesh and two grays
Size: 20″ by 25″

Beaux Arts Ball, Hope College

When a client three states away calls late Thursday and wants camera-ready art for a poster, three colors-hand separated, by the following Monday at 5 p.m., the designer, to say the least, must move pretty fast—and, if possible, use any existing art that is reasonably appropriate. Designer Lanny Sommese was lucky when he got a call from the De Pree Art Center of Hope College in Holland, Michigan, with just such a request for a poster announcing its Beaux Arts Ball. Sommese happened to have been working on an idea for a possible Graphis cover that seemed ideal for the rush assignment.

Hope College had one other stipulation: the poster was to be 17½″ by 23¼″, the maximum capability of the local Michigan printer.

The time limitation and need for hand-separation dictated a simple approach. Sommese's concept was a devil with artist's brushes driven down through his head so that pointed handles become horns and brush tips become fangs protruding from the mouth. Despite the horns and fangs, the devil has a rather jolly look, holding out the promise of a "fun" evening.

The tissue drawing was executed in heavy black ink, then parts of the black were erased by painting over in white to produce a stained-glass look. This would result in bold dark lines filled with color on the finished poster, in the style of Georges Roualt or Piatti.

The colors were brownish red, blue and yellow. The paint brush horns and fangs were all supposed to be yellow with yellow and blue bristles. Sommese, who saw no proofs, was startled when he finally received copies of the poster to discover that the right-hand "horn" was green instead. In his haste with the separations, working on black-and-white overlays, he had failed to remove the blue from the yellow in that spot. "If I'd seen a proof, it wouldn't have happened," he says. "But now I like it. It provides an interesting spatial change."

Left: Sketches the artist had been working on in connection with another possible assignment.

Client: De Pree Art Center, Hope College, Holland, MI
Art director/designer/illustrator: Lanny Sommese
Printer: Steketee-Van Huys Printers, Inc.
Colors: Blue, yellow, red
Size: 17½″ by 23¼″
Printer: Steketee-Van Huys Printers
Colors: Blue, yellow, red
Size: 17½″ by 23¼″

April Fool Film Festival

For close to a decade, Bruce Bedinger's April Fool Film Festival of TV and radio advertising out-takes and goofs has been eagerly awaited by those in the Chicago area who appreciate that sort of thing. Since people who savor what the festival calls advertising atrocities constitute a literate audience, its perpetrators feel their promotion can be strange and funky as well as funny.

When Bedinger, a VP/creative director of Foote Cone & Belding in Chicago, started the festival in 1976, he held it in his home. But it outgrew those quarters and since 1979 has been held in a local restaurant, with David Bartels designing the poster announcing the event. Bartels says that, every year, he and Alex Murawski, who has done the illustrations for five years, swear they'll never do another one of these "labors of love." "In fact," he threatens, "we're going to call the next one 'The Last.'"

"Since we decide a year ahead what we're going to do," relates Murawski, "I had plenty of time, after David suggested a devil, to discard one idea after another, hoping to come up with a good one. I did sketch after sketch of devils and they got worse and worse. Finally, my wife, Darlyne, said, 'You've always liked topsy-turvy—why not do one of the devil?' So I was saved by a 19th-century idea. It took about three minutes to design my 'topsy' after weeks of getting nowhere."

Since the poster would be fairly small, 15″ by 30″, Murawski wanted to keep the image simple. And since the budget (or lack of it) dictated only two colors, it would need dramatic highlighting—in two directions. "As it turned out," he says, "the simple color treatment set off the art. The high-contrast stage lighting gives it punch. One way it's very spooky, and the other way it's benign. Putting the headline both right side up and upside down forces you to turn it over to see the other face." The two-way devil, black on a mauve background, does indeed offer contrasts. The reverse of the goofy, glaring devil resembles a happy-go-lucky Hollywood cartoon animal, of the protruding teeth variety.

Three thousand copies of the poster were lithographed and can still be seen on office and home walls. Admits Murawski, "I use it for self-promotion all the time."

Left: Sketch of poster showing the reverse-image "evil" face.

Client: Bruce Bedinger
Design firm: Bartels & Co., St. Louis
Art director/designer: David Bartels
Designer/illustrator: Alex Murawski
Printer: Harrison Litho, Inc.
Colors: Black and mauve
Size: 15″ by 30″

First Annual Designers' Chili Cookoff

The poster which kicked off the now-annual Designers' Chili Cookoff in Dallas was the contribution of Dennard Creative, Inc., the folks who thought up the cookoff idea one day as they were having lunch at a local chili restaurant. At first, they were only going to invite their own clients, but then decided to see if competing graphic design firms would like to join them as hosts. There were five takers for the first event, held in the fall of 1981 at Big John's, a dude ranch. "About 1000 designers and their clients and friends turned up the first year," reports Bob Dennard, head of Dennard Creative, "and it was a real happening. We had 3000 the next year and almost 5000 in 1983."

For people not familiar with the goings-on in chili country, a cookoff, or, anyway, the designers' cookoff, works this way: Contestants set up booths, prepare their chili and cook it on a portable camp gas stove. When the official judges come around, the cooks present their chili in an entertaining way—with a speech, poem, song, dance, or whatever. Meanwhile, the crowd is entertained with music, a hayride, games and contests. Then everybody eats chili.

"Since it was our idea," says Dennard, "we got to do the poster." In a long, narrow format (17″ by 36″), Rex Peteet designed a festive bright red jalapeña pepper with a light green stem on a background of chili green for the top two-thirds, bright yellow below that. Oval slices of the pepper fall in a series of bright pastel geometric designs that aren't Mexican, but give the feeling of Mexican folk art. The final oval is solid blue on yellow.

"Actually," says Dennard, "the designs are nonsensical graphic scribblings, sort of New Wave 'noodles' with, we hope, a Dallas twist. We took from everywhere for the fun of it. There's a Salvadore Dali look to the pepper floating against a green 'sky' over the horizon of a yellow 'plain.' The blue oval is the shadow. The hand-designed type at the top looks suspiciously like Milton Glaser's Baby Fat." One thousand posters were lithographed in seven flat and two process colors on Mohawk Superfine ivory.

Client/design firm: Dennard Creative, Inc., Dallas
Art directors: Bob Dennard, Rex Peteet
Designer/illustrator/letterer: Rex Peteet
Printer: Yaquinto Printing Co.
Colors: Seven flat pastels, two process
Size: 17″ by 36″

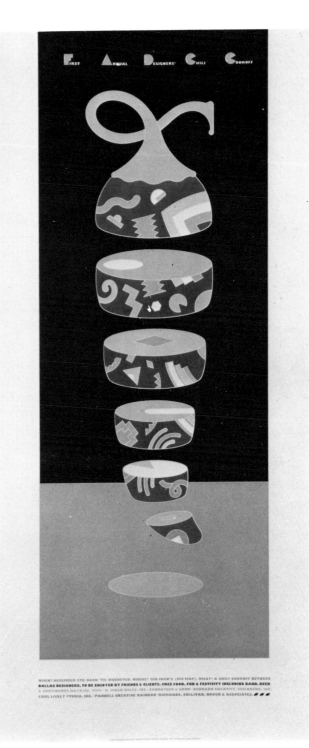

I Remember Nelson

The Masterpiece Theater dramatization, *I Remember Nelson*, portrayed segments of Admiral Horatio Nelson's life from different points of view, including those of his wife, a subordinate officer and a common sailor. Before he began to paint, Paul Davis, who was commissioned by its underwriter, Mobil Oil Corporation, to design a poster announcing the PBS-aired TV series, viewed all of the episodes showing the heroic, romantic and public sides of the hero of the Battle of Trafalgar (in which he was killed). "But you can't portray a character from all points of view," says Davis. "You have to narrow it down. Otherwise, it would just be a montage. Successful posters show only a moment, or are symbolic."

Mobil provided Davis with background information and photographs of Kenneth Colley, who played Nelson in the series. The artist also visited the library to do further research and to "look at every portrait of Nelson I could find." "I discovered," he says, "that Nelson led a bizarre and interesting life. Like a lot of historical figures, he was a real loony. Also, every portrait of him was completely romanticized; they made him look pretty, like those portrait photos in the '50s where you knew no one really looked like that."

Davis found a symbolic Nelson, heroic and romantic— and even a little loony. The perspective from below gives heroic stature and emphasizes the gold buttons and braid on the uniform and enormous admiral's hat, the empty sleeve

and scar over one eye. To fit this Admiral Nelson—no pretty boy—Davis hand-lettered the type in a classical face that "echoes World War I recruitment images, the last of those super-patriotic, sabre-rattling American posters."

The 30″-by-46″ poster was displayed in subways and in commuter train and bus stations. It also was enlarged for bus shelter art in New York City and adapted for black-and-white newspaper and magazine ads.

Client: Mobil Oil Corp., New York City
Creative director: Sandra Ruch
Designer/illustrator: Paul Davis
Copywriter: Fran Michelman
Printer: Crafton Printing Co.
Colors: Four-color process
Size: 30″ by 46″

USA Film Festival

For the 1983 USA Film Festival—held, as usual, in Dallas—the client wanted the Texas location to be prominent in a poster that, besides publicizing the festival, would be presented to celebrity guests and film studio people and be offered for sale at this 11th annual event. It also would be reproduced on the program book.

Since the funds of the non-profit festival were limited, a black-and-white photograph seemed the best solution. Kent Kirkley, who agreed to do the poster photography for expenses-only because of his long-time interest in the film festival, presented a number of ideas. Selected because of its Texas flavor was the image of a Pony Express rider delivering a reel of film. Kirkley rented a western outfit for a model who had her own horse. Then he photographed her with two cameras as she rode by on a country road carrying an old aluminum film reel, chrome-plated so it would show up, with film streaming off the reel. Actually, the model had complained about carrying the 20-pound reel, so Kirkley made a black-and-white print of the full reel, removed the film and replaced it with the photo cut to size, then attached just enough film to give the streamer effect. "I thought this first effort was too blurred," he reports. "I figured that, to get the ethereal look I wanted, I had shot at too slow a speed." There was another session a few weeks later, but the faster speed resulted in a hard look and too much detail, so he went back to the first film.

For art direction, Kirkley called on Jill Hawkins, with whom he often worked. Hawkins suggested using several photos to simulate a strip of movie film. "Since I had shot for my original idea of a single image," reports Kirkley, "it took some doing to find three prints that we could get away with putting together. Actually, the change between them is not really imperceptible as it should be, but it's interesting because of that."

To achieve the look of an enlarged film strip, Kirkley first shot a piece of film with sprocket holes. Prestype was used to make the festival title look like printing on the outside edge, and then it was rephotographed. The printer reversed out the letters and blew up the sprocket photo to match the size of the stills and stripped them together. A brown-black and blue-black in the duotone created the desired effect.

"As more and more time went into this expenses-only project," says Kirkley, "I kept telling myself that, anyway, this would be a nice photo to have my name on. P.S. my name was misspelled."

Left: Alternate poster idea.

Client: USA Film Festival, Dallas
Art director: Jill Hawkins
Designers: Jill Hawkins, Kent Kirkley
Photographer: Kent Kirkley
Printer: Brodnax Printing Co.
Colors: Brown-black and neutral (blue) black duotone
Size: 23″ wide, left side 27¼″, right side 36″

Intimate Architecture

As the focal point of an exhibition on 20th-century fashion design, the MIT Committee on the Visual Arts invited the participation of eight clothing designers "whose skills are those of builders rather than decorators." Clothes by these designers were displayed in the show at the Hayden Gallery and photographs of their designs were featured, some humorously, in the exhibition catalog.

Curator Susan Sidlauskas commissioned art photographer Robert Mapplethorpe, who had never done fashion work, to take the black-and-white catalog photos because she felt that "his handling of black, gray and white was subtle and elegant." The humor was to lie in the fact that the model, Lisa Lyons, who has written a book on body-building, was muscular and thus unlike the "anorexic" fashion models she parodies. Although the muscles, dark underarm hair and earthy poses of the model in some pictures certainly parody the glamorous photos of Irving Penn, Richard Avedon and Cecil Beaton, they are tame for an audience exposed to the bizarre and/or kinky fashion photos of, say, Helmut Newton and Deborah Turbeville. In fact, the photo used for the catalog cover and poster is so demure, a few of the pictures inside the catalog come as a shock.

Mapplethorpe cropped this photo so that legs and shoes disappear into the black background and only the shadowed bottom of the model's face shows. The back-buttoned white merino coat piped in black (by Yeohlee Teng) hangs free in folds that make a wavy

hem line. Jacqueline Casey of the MIT Design Services, who designed the catalog and poster, chose to show the photo horizontally, on the right in the poster with copy at the left. "Vertical treatment on the poster, with type at the bottom," she points out, "would have made it look like a fashion ad. This way the ragged line of the flush-left copy mirrors the image of the hem. It's absolutely married to the hem line." To achieve the same quality as the original photograph, the poster was printed as a black duotone—black ink and PMS 407 gray—and given a matte varnish on the third run.

Above: One of Robert Mapplethorpe's photos of model/body-builder Lisa Lyons from the exhibition catalog.

Client: MIT Committee on the Visual Arts, Cambridge, MA
Design firm: MIT Design Services
Art director/designer: Jacqueline S. Casey
Photographer: Robert Mapplethorpe
Copywriter: Susan Sidlauskas
Printer: Arlington Lithographic Co.
Colors: Black (with gray) duotone
Size: 29″ by 23″

Le Train Bleu

Shortly after it opened an upscale French restaurant named Le Train Bleu in its flagship Manhattan store, Bloomingdale's decided the entrance area to the new eating spot didn't have enough impact. They turned to Michael Doret, who had designed the restaurant logo and illustrated a menu cover which captured the spirit of Bloomingdale's tribute to the 1930s trains of the French railroad system. The restaurant is designed as a long, narrow train dining room with windows on one side looking out on the city scene. Doret's menu cover evokes the 1930s era with its impeccable stylization of all elements—letterforms, train and a city landscape dominated by the Chrysler building. A sliver of moon hangs in the sky.

Doret was asked to design two seven-foot-high illuminated panels which would flank the staircase to the restaurant. The only stipulation: the signing panels must conform to the tone of the menu cover. Doret did an 8½"-by-31" airbrush painting in gouache which is much simpler and more powerful than his previous illustration. Whereas the menu train is rather fat and friendly and is named "Bloomingdale's," the train in the panel is sleek, dangerous, bullet-shaped and speeding directly at the viewer, its headlights sweeping through the night. The same moon, though, appears in the upper-right-hand corner.

Doret's painting was blown up for the right-hand panel and flopped to produce the mirror image on the left. "This was a challenge," Doret recalls. "Since it was being enlarged to seven feet, I had to paint extremely tight. Also, I usually work in pre-separated art, and here I had to produce a piece of reflective art."

Later, the art (Doret had retained the rights) was published as a fine art poster by ProCreations Publishing of New Orleans. The painting was translated into pre-separated art and lithographed in 10 impressions with Pantone inks. The long train in two shades of blue rides on a panel of gray and gray-green, while the letters at the top are placed in a color block of rose shading to plum and dropped out in the "Cassandre" squash yellow that forms the border.

Above: Michael Doret's logo and menu cover for Bloomingdale's Le Train Bleu restaurant. Logo was made into a three-dimensional wooden plaque outside restaurant and printed on china and other service items.

Client: ProCreations Publishing, New Orleans
Designer/illustrator/letterer: Michael Doret, New York City
Printer: Miller & Sons
Colors: 10 PMS
Size: 8½" by 32"

This Violent Century

John Sorbie wanted to create a "strong, brutal image" for the poster announcing a Colorado State University presentation of outstanding films on war and social and political conflict. Titled "This Violent Century," the film series was sponsored by the CSU Office of Cultural Programs. The films ranged from *Grand Illusion* of the 1930s to such fairly recent releases as *Gallipoli.*

"The budget dictated one-color printing and line art only," says Sorbie, "while the size was limited both by local press capabilities and campus posting area regulations." Sorbie began by making a 5″-by-8″ pencil drawing of sheet metal with rivets and punch perforations. "I smeared the pencil lines with my thumb," he says, "to get a gray, halftone look." Then, he enlarged the drawing into a 12″-by-18″ halftone with a vertical line screen and made three or four copies. Next, he cut the stats into pieces and reassembled them on black paper. He cut some pieces to specific shapes to make the profile of a helmeted soldier and a couple of swastikas. The result is an unsettling collage, with the look of Dada or the Italian Futurists, that shouts war and devastation. The little faces here and there that seem to be peering out from behind barbed wire were, says Sorbie, completely inadvertent—"they just appeared." The black letters of the title look as though they had been riddled by shot. To achieve this effect, Sorbie put down Prestype, then applied a piece of masking tape. When he removed the tape, some of the type came off with it, giving a look of disintegration to the remainder.

"I was after the strength you see in European movie posters, especially in Poland," Sorbie reports. "The Polish posters are tough stuff. They're not commercial and they've got guts. American movie posters are soft; everybody is in on the solution from the director to the guy who sweeps out the theater."

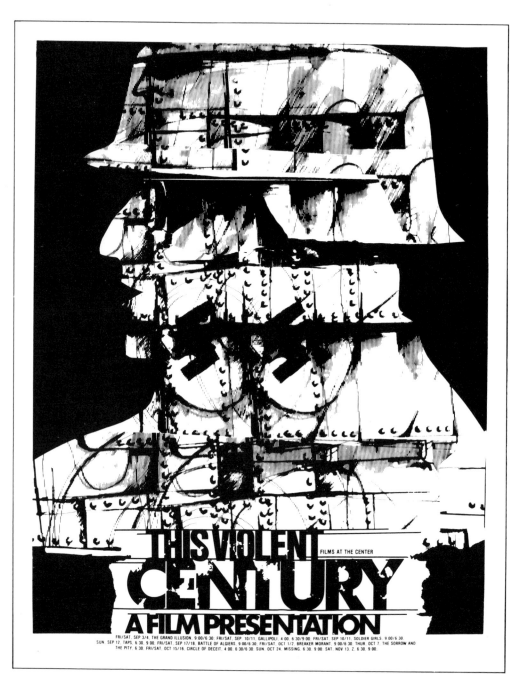

Client: Office of Cultural Programs, Colorado State University, Ft. Collins
Design firm: Sorbie Roche Design
Art director/designer/illustrator: John Sorbie
Printer: Citizens Printing
Colors: Black-and-white
Size: 23″ by 29″

Halloween Block Party

The block between 1177 and 1189 Virginia Avenue, N.E., in Atlanta, Georgia, is the business address of a number of architects, photographers, designers and advertising agencies, along with what this group calls "normal" people. Since the late '70s, occupants of the block have donated the fruits of their particular talent to the success of a big Halloween costume block party for themselves and friends and clients in the Atlanta area.

Since people had started coming to the parties without costumes, or using the lack of a costume as an excuse for staying away, Jerry Sullivan of Sullivan and/or Haas Designers decided to print the 1982 poster invitation on a large (12″ by 18″) brown paper grocery bag which could be worn on the head as a costume of sorts. He asked artist Bill Mayer, who had done a number of the previous posters, to come up with "something crazy and scary" for an illustration. Mayer quickly made a 1½″ line drawing of a bug-eyed, snaggle-toothed cartoony character. This was blown up 400 per cent to fill the top of the folded bag.

One thousand bags were silkscreened in dark blue and pink with opaque ink so the colors wouldn't run. They became mailers when they were folded with the image inside and labels attached. "Three thousand people came with bags on their heads," says Mayer. "People who didn't have a poster just used any old bag."

Left: Original thumbnail drawing which was blown up to poster size.

Client: Virginia Ave. Block Party, Atlanta
Design firm: Sullivan and/or Haas
Art director: Jerry Sullivan
Designers: Jerry Sullivan, Bill Mayer
Illustrator: Bill Mayer
Copywriter: Ken Haas
Printer: Process Posters
Colors: Blue, pink
Size: 12″ by 18″

The merger of two New England companies known for their adherence to high standards of printing and reproduction occasioned a two-panel poster by designer Lance Hidy, a friend and associate of management of both the Meriden Gravure Company of Meriden, Connecticut, and the Stinehour Press, Lunenburg, Vermont.

Hidy was commissioned by Roderick Stinehour, president of Meriden-Stinehour, Inc., to design a poster that would clarify the merger in the minds of customers and friends of the two companies. Stephen Harvard of the Stinehour Press, a book designer, lettering artist and graphic arts historian, suggested using two panels with the image continuing across both, a device used by Utamaro and other Japanese printmakers.

As is his custom, Hidy worked from his own photos, shooting about four rolls at each plant, mostly color slides. From the photographs he made drawings, and then started introducing color, taking six months to develop the colors and the composition. The left (Meriden) panel came early, based on a photo of Stephen Stinehour, manager at Meriden, holding a sheet of paper which crosses over into the other panel, symbolizing the merger.

On the Stinehour panel, there were few problems with the main image, modeled on Stinehour pressroom foreman John McCormack locking (or unlocking?) a form. But the background took time. Hidy first used a window, intended to indicate a rural New England setting. The window evolved

into an alphabet such as Stephen Harvard makes, carved in black slate and gilded. Harvard, vice-president of Meriden-Stinehour, did the lettering for the alphabet and for the poster titles.

The image was printed by offset lithography at Meriden, in eight mixed-to-match flat colors resulting in shades of yellow, gray and burnt orange accented by black and white. Fade-resistant pigments on acid-free paper, Monadnock Dulcet, should insure long life. One thousand posters were printed, each panel measuring 10″ by 30″. Since there was extra room on the sheet, the panels were printed in two smaller sizes, 11″ and 6¾″ deep, for use in various company mailings.

Right: Photos taken by artist Lance Hidy on which to base his poster drawings. Far right: Stinehour pressroom foreman John McCormack with printing form. Other photo shows manager Stephen Stinehour inspecting printed sheet.

Client: Meriden-Stinehour, Inc., Meriden, CT, and Lunenburg, VT
Art directors: Stephen Harvard, Roderick Stinehour
Designer/illustrator: Lance Hidy
Letterer/copywriter: Stephen Harvard
Printer: Meriden-Stinehour
Colors: Eight mixed-to-match
Size: Two 10″ by 30″ panels

Since the shoppers at Conran's housewares and home furnishings stores are more sophisticated than department or chain store customers, designer Cheryl Lewin felt she could venture a Christmas poster that would bring a new perspective to an ancient holiday. "I wanted something less literal and more provocative," she says, "a way to make people view Christmas differently." She found in Dagmar Frinta's decorative, multi-patterned, folk-image St. Nicholas "the charm and whimsy appropriate to Conran's, as well as a sophistication and elegance."

Working in gouache and watercolors with Cello-Tak applied on sepia paper, Frinta created a portly, grandfatherly man in pointed stocking cap, pensively holding a mug of what—a fanciful tiny tree and candy canes tell us—can only be some kind of "Christmas cheer." His costume, even his beard, is made of row upon row and layer upon layer of different fabrics. The colors are dark and somber—there's no beaming, red-capped Santa Claus here— but the holiday spirit comes across. "As usual when I do a decorative piece," says Frinta, "I just started playing with patterns and colors, the way Persian paintings deal with fabrics and carpets. I got the contour of the head by modeling tissue paper until I found the shape I wanted."

The posters were displayed in Conran's U.S. stores during the two-month Christmas retail season in 1981 and picked up for the European (Habitat) stores in 1982. They were also used for subway posters in London.

Client: Conran's, New York City
Art director/designer: Cheryl Lewin
Illustrator: Dagmar Frinta
Printer: Davis Printing
Colors: Four-color process
Size: 17″ by 22″

Citivues: New York, Boston

Several years ago, illustrator Albert Lorenz was retained by the Gips & Balkind design firm to do isometric drawings of lower and midtown Manhattan, to be used as promotion pieces for a real estate firm. The drawings were astonishing in their meticulous detail and scope—so large that they showed the curvature of the earth—and were chosen by the Casebooks 5 jurors for their beauty as well as their technique.

Lorenz was so fascinated by the assignment that he later redid the drawings, updating them, adding details, refining others. He then went on to make drawings of other of the world's interesting cities, had a poster format designed, dubbed them Citivues, and launched a campaign to market them. He submitted posters for eight cities (there now are 10) to Casebooks 6; the jurors called them all extraordinary but preferred those for New York and Boston.

Working from wide-angle and regular-lens aerial photographs, site plans and architectural drawings, Lorenz uses pen-and-ink on 30″ by 40″ bristol board to give him the largest feasible original. The unusual perspective and the painstaking detail of a whole city's major buildings and landmarks available in one glance remove them from the realm of typical architectural drawings. It takes Lorenz about 200 hours to finish one drawing, even though—"to keep me sane"— he has others do the tedious stippling.

The posters were printed full-size on white cover stock in dark blue on tan with a narrow

NEW YORK

HOUSTON

SAN FRANCISCO

BOSTON

red, white and blue "airmail envelope" border and a couple of paragraphs in small type at the top describing the history and magic of each city.

Lorenz printed 5000 of each poster, which he originally intended as guides to the city as well as graphic art. However, they don't work as a practical guide because they lack identifying information and they soon become slightly outdated by the construction pace in some cities. Lorenz hopes, therefore, to sell them as graphics through poster stores and museum shops.

Below, opposite page and this page: In addition to the Casebook-selected posters for New York (midtown and lower Manhattan) and Boston, the series includes Houston, San Francisco, Toronto, and Chicago.

Client/illustrator: Albert Lorenz, Floral Park, NY
Art direction/design/copy: Citivues
Printer: C.G.S., Inc.
Colors: Red, blue, tan
Size: 30″ by 40″

As a goodwill gesture to some of its builders and suppliers, Paul Broadhead & Associates, a Dallas-based developer of shopping malls, decided to invite them to have brunch and attend a professional football game. Broadhead asked Dennard Creative, Inc., to produce a lighthearted invitation that would impress its prospective guests in Atlanta, Georgia, and insure a good turnout.

Dennard proceeded to find its solution the way it usually does, through an inter-office "competition." In more of a free-for-all of ideas than an actual contest, the Dennard designers all come up with roughs of their concept, then, by critiquing themselves, reach a consensus on the best solution. If it seems that several will work, they are presented to the client to choose. But Dennard is not required to provide alternatives and generally uses the one selected internally.

The "winner" in this case was a poster-invitation, Rex Peteet's geometric design in bright pastels of a referee blowing his whistle under the title "Time-Out," chosen for its double application to football and to a break from work. The referee, in lavender pants and lavender and white striped shirt, is a series of angles resulting from bent arms, knees and elongated feet. The background is a football field indicated by a series of vertically stacked, three-dimensional "10-yard" segments in dark and light green. Letters of the title, hand-drawn in red with green drop shadows, are placed on round disks—yellow

with light purple shadows. The letters travel up to a peak and back down, outlining the angle of the referee's raised arms.

"It's a designer's illustration," says Bob Dennard. "The whole thing works together—the type, the background, the negative and positive elements. Each part is related, whereas a traditional illustration is a separate entity. The positioning of Peteet's referee with his T-squared angles points to everything else."

Originally scheduled for silkscreening, the poster was lithographed when the client doubled the press run by deciding to use it, with copy changes, to invite Dallas people to a game there.

Client: Paul Broadhead & Associates, Inc., Dallas
Design firm: Dennard Creative, Dallas
Art directors: Bob Dennard, Rex Peteet
Designer/illustrator: Rex Peteet
Colors: Dark green, light green, purple, lavender, red, yellow, blue
Size: 19½" by 34"

The Dallas Society of Visual Communications planned to show the 1982 Clio-award-winning TV commercials in a movie theater that still had its original Art Deco décor. Also, commercials from the 1960s would be shown along with the 1982 winners. Basing his solution on those two "givens," Glyn Boyd of Dennard Creative designed a playful poster invitation combining TV commercial characters of the '60s with an Art Deco movie theater facade.

Festive, bright pastel colors are enclosed in silver lines that vary in width from narrow for the ones that outline mosaic to heavier for the ones delineating two packages set up like movie posters. One is a milk carton with Elsie the Cow and her pitcher of milk on the front, the other an Alka-Seltzer package featuring the boy with the wand. Centered between these "posters" is a ticket booth decorated as a parody of Deco excesses. The ticket-seller is a silly Jolly Green Giant whose "Ho, Ho, Ho!" wafts along on silver letters. The pale green leaves of his hat and Tarzan outfit are outlined in silver.

Boyd says he drew in pen on newsprint because that makes the ink bleed, creating an interesting line. The bright red title letters were done with a Rapidograph and drop-shadowed. The silver lines were laid down last in opaque ink "to cover up where the seven PMS colors didn't always come together."

Client: Dallas Society of Visual Communications
Design firm: Dennard Creative, Inc., Dallas
Art director: Bob Dennard
Designer/illustrator/letterer: Glyn Boyd
Printer: Yaquinto Printing Co.
Colors: Seven PMS colors plus silver
Size: 22½" by 36"

Presented by the Dallas Society of Visual Communications. Free to members. Non-members $2.00. Enter through The Lounge at the Inwood Theater. Cash bar. Cocktails at 6. Continuous showing of 1982 and 1960 Clios starting at 7:30.

Grand Central

In 1963, Aline Saarinen, Philip Johnson, Ulrich Franzen and a very few other architects and citizens who care about preserving our architectural heritage picketed alone in the snow to try to save New York City's Pennsylvania Station. They lost that battle, but learned a lesson. By 1965, they had joined with others to establish the city's Landmarks Preservation Commission, which named Grand Central Terminal a landmark. When builders tried to overturn the designation and erect a 55-story building over the Beaux Arts treasure, a committee to save Grand Central was formed which worked with other civic groups in helping the city take the matter to the U.S. Supreme Court. There, in 1978, after a 10-year legal battle, the landmark status was upheld.

This long struggle added special zest to the celebration of Grand Central's 70th birthday in 1983. The Municipal Art Society of New York started early with an exhibition of Grand Central memorabilia and publication of a hard-cover book about the terminal. Keith Godard of Works designed the book and, with Jeri Froehlich, did the superb cover illustration which was used for the exhibition's poster and catalog cover. Seeking a "surreal fantasy" solution, Godard hit on the idea of a mixed-period painting of the surrounding cityscape with Grand Central rising in all its lovingly-detailed Beaux Arts splendor high above the pared-down shapes of the other buildings. The gray, yellow, orange and black of Froehlich's Plaka painting are right out of the Braque-Picasso

  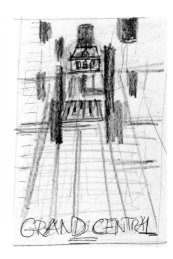

  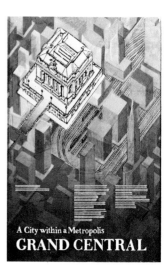

Above: Preliminary overall and detail sketches, drawings and paintings. Right: Keith Godard's line drawing of Grand Central terminal. Opposite page left: With paper engineer Robin Bernstein, Godard designed a kit for building a replica of Grand Central with instructions "do not lose" on the smallest pieces.

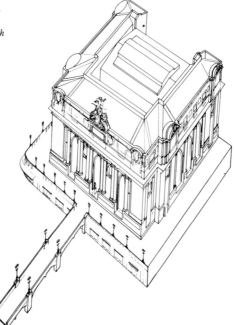

Cubist works that were beginning to acquire an audience when Grand Central was built in 1913. The style in which she depicted the other buildings, and the trains and tracks laid bare in Grand Central's underworld, is pure late '20s/early '30s, the era of the Chrysler Building across the street from the terminal. By contrast, Godard's line drawing of Grand Central (done on an overlay and tinted by the printer) is detailed enough to make out the time on the clock under the statues of Mercury, Hercules and Minerva on the 42nd Street facade.

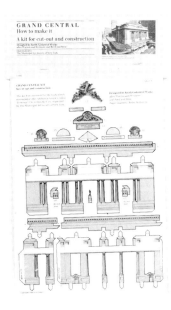

Client: Municipal Art Society of New York; funding sponsors: Philip Morris, Inc; National Endowment for the Humanities
Design firm: Works, New York City
Designers: Keith Godard, assisted by Jeri Froehlich
Copywriter: Deborah Nevins (curator)
Printer: Georgian Press
Colors: Four-color process
Size: 24″ by 38″

GRAND CENTRAL
TERMINAL
City within the City

An exhibition organized by The Municipal Art Society, sponsored by Philip Morris Incorporated and the National Endowment for the Humanities, with additional funding provided by the National Endowment for the Arts

The New-York Historical Society
170 Central Park West, at 77th St.
New York City

May 27th to September 13th, 1982

Introducing Connections

Approached by Simpson Paper Company to help revitalize its image, Cross Associates, as part of a larger program, came up with the idea for a series of posters by 24 distinguished designers and illustrators, printed, of course, on Simpson paper.

Simpson is the largest manufacturer of uncoated printing paper in the U.S., with 25 per cent of the market, but most designers didn't know that because the company had promoted itself primarily to printers rather than to the people at agencies and design firms who specify paper.

In addition to the poster series, which began a two-year schedule in the fall of 1982, Cross Associates produced books containing techniques for using Simpson uncoated papers to reproduce photographs and illustrations. The poster series is called "Connections" and designers were given complete latitude in expressing that theme. Some were personal (Seymour Chwast's comb and toothbrush), others more formal (Rudolph de Harak's spatial grid drawing). Ivan Chermayeff collaged a woman's face with torn bits of paper, including masking tape. The only stipulations were the convenient 20″ by 28″ size and use of the title—in widely spaced sans-serif letters—and a punchy three-word Simpson blurb. Each poster also carries a statement (devised with the help of Cross copywriters) from the designers or illustrators on what the term "connections" means to them.

Cross Associates launched the series with a poster introducing the 24 participants by printing their signatures, each on a torn swatch of paper. The variously colored and textured papers were arranged according to design and photographed in full color, the signatures overprinted. The Casebook jurors chose the introductory poster because it was straightforward, clean and simple. The signatures, on lusciously colored paper, made a personal statement and

created anticipation for the series.

James Cross, head of Cross Associates, said he could only judge the impact of the series by the requests that increased the client's mailing list from 5000 to 13,000 and by the success of a new line of Simpson's linen finish paper called Filare. Introduced in the East about eight months after the posters first appeared, and bolstered by a Cross ad and promotion campaign, the new line sold as much in the first three months as had been projected for the first year.

Left: Early preliminary tissue sketch with names intermixed.

Client: Simpson Paper Co., San Francisco
Design firm: Cross Associates, Newport Beach, CA
Art director: James Cross
Designers: James Cross, Steve Martin
Photographer: Jim Porter
Printer: Gardner/Fulmer Lithograph
Colors: Four-color process
Size: 20″ by 24″

March for the Dream

Asked to contribute a poster for the 20th anniversary march on Washington in the summer of 1983, designer/illustrator Fred Marcellino wanted to find an image that would cut across political lines and appeal to all Americans. Despite the exhortatory sound of the slogan: "March for the Dream: Jobs, Peace, Freedom," Marcellino knew that the diverse groups sponsoring the march were trying to appeal to the broadest possible range of potential participants. They needed the poster for fund-raising prior to the march commemorating Martin Luther King, Jr.'s "I have a dream" speech and as a general call for attendance.

"I didn't want to deal with symbols associated with liberal causes, like doves and guitars," reports Marcellino. "Since the right had co-opted most of the patriotic images—the flag, for instance—I thought we ought to start getting them back and why not start with the Statue of Liberty?" Marcellino found a simple, moving way to convey a complexity of ideas. The poster recreates in the foreground the scene of the first march, the crowd—banners raised— gathered around the pool in front of the Washington Monument, the Capitol in the distance. Dawn is breaking, and rising with the sun is the Statue of Liberty, stars from the still-dark-blue sky at the top shining around her head and across her disconcertingly steadfast eyes.

Marcellino airbrushed his painting, putting in details by hand with brush and acrylic. The hand-lettering, dropped out in white, is meant to evoke "a little bit of the feeling of political and labor posters of the '30s."

Cost considerations dictated that the intended run of 25,000 posters be printed four-color process offset. Two hundred and fifty posters were printed on fine paper, some signed by the artist and by King's widow, Coretta Scott King, and auctioned.

Client: Arms Control Computer Network, Washington, DC
Designer/illustrator: Fred Marcellino
Printer: Clements Printing Co.
Colors: Four-color process
Size: 18″ by 26″

Stravinsky

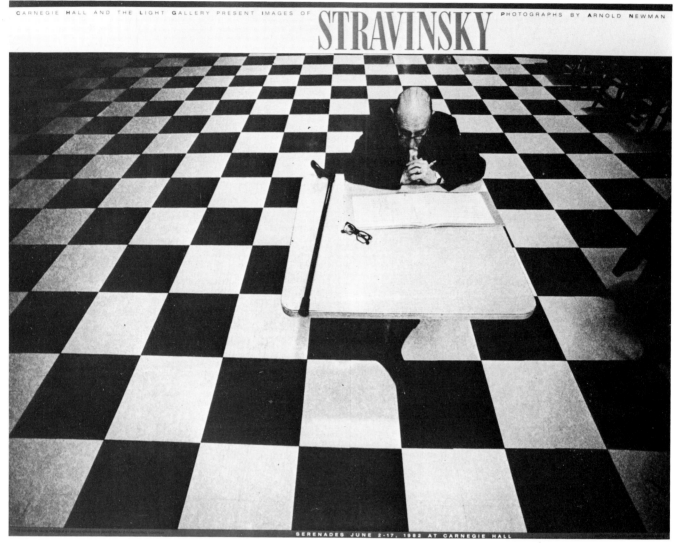

CARNEGIE HALL AND THE LIGHT GALLERY PRESENT IMAGES OF **STRAVINSKY** PHOTOGRAPHS BY ARNOLD NEWMAN

SERENADES JUNE 2-17, 1982 AT CARNEGIE HALL

For a poster announcing an exhibition of Arnold Newman's photographs of Igor Stravinsky at the Light Gallery—celebrating the composer's 100th birthday—and a concurrent series of concerts at Carnegie Hall featuring Stravinsky's music, Tibor Kalman of M&Co. chose one of Newman's horizontal photos, keeping the typography simple so that the picture could speak for itself.

The striking photograph shows Stravinsky sitting at a small table, absorbed in studying a music score. The figure is alone on a vast floor of large black-and-white squares that could be marble, terrazzo, vinyl or even carpet. (Actually, it was the vinyl floor of a rehearsal room in the Henry Hudson Hotel in New York City.) Stravinsky's air of total concentration is almost intimidating, while his bald head, aging hands, cane and glasses give evidence of mortality that fill the viewer with warmth and compassion.

"The beautiful Newman photograph was cropped perfectly," says Kalman. "So, rather than reduce the photo, we designed it to run as large as possible." The single word "Stravinsky" in large, compressed Bodoni type, printed in purple, is placed off-center (directly over the composer) on a 2″ white strip with a ¼″ black border running across the top. On a ⅜″ red strip across the bottom—in Helvetica Extended Regular and Bold—appear the dates of the Carnegie Hall serenades (white type) and a notice (black type) that the photo exhibition was underwritten by City Investing Company.

The large (30″ by 23″) format was chosen to stand out from the mostly vertical posters announcing Carnegie Hall events. Kalman was pleased with the outcome, calling it a "literary, lyrical and highly graphic poster." The Casebook jurors agreed.

Client: Carnegie Hall, New York City; Tom Baker, marketing manager
Design firm: M&Co., New York City
Art directors/designers: Tibor Kalman, Carol Bokuniewicz
Copywriter: Tom Baker
Photographer: Arnold Newman
Printer: Eastern Press
Colors: Red, two blacks
Size: 30″ by 23″